Fluffy Muffins

Fluffy Muffins

Recipes for My Peeps

Susanna Lee

Rose Mason Press

Douglassville, PA USA

10 9 8 7 6 5 4 3 2 1

Rose Mason Press, an imprint of HPL Publications,
PO Box 564, Douglassville, PA 19518
USA

ISBN: 978-1-61305-034-7

Library of Congress Control Number: 2021952105

Library of Congress Cataloging-in-Publication Data

Lee, Susanna, 1956 –
Fluffy Muffins / Susanna Lee
        p. cm.
ISBN: 978-1-61305-034-7
I. Title
PS3621.M84L44
811'.6-dc23   2021952105

Summary: Close observation captures moments in poetry.

Subjects: Poetry; Poetry -- Authorship; Lee, Susanna --
Poetry; American poetry -- 21st century.

Tags: poetry, American poetry.

Cover photo by Susanna Lee.

Dedication

To those who bring food to family parties.

CONTENTS

How to Cook

The Recipes

THE RECIPES (CONT.)

THE RECIPES (CONT.)

THE RECIPES (CONT.)

The Recipes (cont.)

THE RECIPES (CONT.)

MEAT AND CHEESE (CONT.)

FILLING, PUDDING, SAUCES, TOPPINGS, ICING

PARTY DRINKS – VIRGIN (NO ALCOHOL)

PARTY DRINKS – ADULT (CONTAINS ALCOHOL)

THE RECIPES (CONT.)

PARTY DRINKS – ADULT (CONTAINS ALCOHOL) (CONT.)

LA PIÈCE DE RÉSISTANCE

Preface

Food. Good, now I've finally got it all written down in this book. Even if I go blind, I can still tell my peeps how to make my favorite recipes. So far, I'm in perfect health, but my grandmother lost her eyesight and lived for decades at the mercy of those who did not know the art of cooking.

In writing this book, I just wanted to give my kids and grandkids a chance to cook what my mom cooked: simple, plain, cheap, nutritious food. And also, to share with those who have no other way to enjoy eating, but find themselves at the mercy of those who prepare their boughten meals.

Good cheap food is quick and easy to make following simple recipes. There is no need to spend a fortune or hours slaving in the kitchen to eat well. That said, there is also no reason to expect that every mouthful will echo with angelic choirs singing the praises of the cook. Keep realistic expectations, then lower those, and you will rarely be disappointed.

My mother was a know-it-all in the kitchen but too busy to share with me any but the basics. She put simple food on the table and said, trust me. Eat this, it's what's good for you.

As I work on this manuscript, I keep in mind my own struggle. I learned a lot about cooking through trial and error, while broke and working 16-hour days. I was hungry and could not afford the time or money for mistakes.

I studied nutrition like erotic fiction, wanting to learn what it means to find satisfaction.

First recommended to me by a friend in college, I started with books by Adele Davis. *Let's Eat Right to Keep Fit* and *Let's Have Healthy Children* gave me an overview of how I could keep myself alive and healthy without my mother there to put good food on the table.

Preparing good food, by yourself, to nourish yourself? What a concept! What a relief, to know it was possible!

Learning how to eat has been a full-time job, a life-long process. For every mile I've run for exercise, I've had to spend at least the same amount of time and effort and determination into putting good nutrients into my body. And it is less of a struggle to show up to exercise than to summon the strength to resist all the bad stuff that everyone else, literally everyone else I know, does not bother trying to resist eating.

A recipe in my book is called, "The Anti-Acne Diet." Eat only that for a lifetime, and it is likely you will not only have healthy skin, but tons of energy and a great mood. It's hard to keep motivated, to stay focused on making good food for yourself. It's easier when you have more energy, which you do get when you "Eat Right to Keep Fit."

My grandmother lived to 102, healthy, eating only healthy food, plus one miniature chocolate, dark chocolate with nuts, after dinner every night.

What helped me was to visualize God walking with me in the supermarket, scrutinizing the choices in the aisles, frowning if I'd put something in my cart I knew I shouldn't. He'd be telling me, in disbelief, "You're not actually going to eat that, are you?! You mean to tell me, I gave you this awesome body, and you're going to screw it over...with JUNK FOOD?!?"

Most of the time I ignore my honest assessment of my value system. Too busy. But as I studied business in the MBA program, I learned how much I'd been manipulated by advertising to make the food choices I make. No one advertises to you to convince you to practice ways to keep in perfect health WHERE THEY WON'T MAKE A DIME OFF YOU.

Other people do make money when we do the food-and-drink things that cause ourselves to live in less than optimal health. If we make poor choices, someone is going to bed richer that night and is not losing sleep over our steadily increasing waistline.

We are not even conscious of the pressures to conform with bad food choices. We happily eat the birthday cake and celebrate every occasion by sharing non-nutritious, or even dangerous, "treats." Happy Halloween! Happy Valentine's Day! Merry Christmas! Were you on Santa's "Nice List"—did he leave you a candy cane in your stocking?

How do you eat right to keep fit today? Some of it is luck. Some is in keeping good company, trusting that people who love you will give you only foods that are good for you. But food processing techniques keep changing, so how would they even know?

It is easy to find people who'd sell you on the idea that what food they offer will make your life easier, or it will be so scrumptious it will give you "flavorgasms" and you won't care if it's nutritious or not.

Learn to make your own bread. Keeping a sourdough alive and thriving will give you insight into what it takes to keep your own body healthy.

Don't wait until you are hungry, plan ahead to eat well. It's like my recipe for sesame bread. If you want to bake sesame bread for tonight's dinner, you have to start by making a "poolish"—twelve hours ago.

This book I included in my "Cubist Poetry Series," a view of my life from all sides at once. Its title, *Fluffy Muffins*, refers to the first recipe I learned in home ec class in high school. Our teacher believed she was teaching us the secret to a lifetime of happiness. She was enthusiastic about sharing the knowledge of how to cook the simple basics, the staples of life. She beamed when our "fluffy muffins" came out of the oven. These cheap, plain muffins would be the stepping stone to our cooking healthy food for ourselves and our families for the rest of our lives. We'd be assured of having good food, enough to be satisfied. We'd be self-sufficient and gain the strength to resist the temptation to let others make our food choices for us. We'd pass down the secret to future generations.

I'm still working at it. I haven't even tested all these recipes.

Susanna Lee, 2021

HOW TO COOK

COOKING BASICS

Family Foods: A First Cookbook

My mother cooked three delicious, nutritious meals for our family every day. She put dinner on the table at five every evening while working full-time, earning her PhD, and picking up eight children from band practice after school. We ate like kings on the salaries of two school teachers. Our red Jell-O had floating bits of fruit cup. We left out for Santa beautifully decorated homemade sugar cookies. Our fresh fruits and vegetables were evidence of my dad's hard labor in our garden.

My dad was so impressed with mom's chocolate cupcakes, he declared, "You've duplicated the Tastycake!" He ate all twelve, leaving none for her bridge club. Mom reminded him that, though she enjoyed creating delicious treats, she was not bound by artificial gender roles to be a slave to her kitchen. If Dad could be satisfied with the Tastycake experience, it would save her time if he would trouble himself to find his cupcakes at ShopRite.

Dad's mother taught my mom her family's recipes for lentil soup and pea soup and stuffed cabbage. Mom often rued the fact that her own mother never allowed anyone into her small kitchen, not even her daughter, so when mom married, her attempts at following a recipe led often to "The Bride's Cake," a disaster due to having no knowledge of the rudiments of cooking. We ate plain food. The spice rack my mom received as a wedding gift was hanging on the wall, the bottles unopened, at her twenty-fifth wedding anniversary. She did not know what to do with any of them.

Mom taught Dad how to make his mother's kidney bean soup soon after the baby went off to college. He was so proud he had "learned to cook."

Truly Great Cooks Share Their Secrets

The author learned to cook from reading and listening to and closely watching and learning from family, friends, books, magazines, newspapers, websites, TV, and the Internet; and then practicing what she learned, adapting ingredients and perfecting techniques to prepare nutritious and delicious food for herself and others.

A very special recognition goes to my in-laws, whose love of delicious food is surpassed only by incredible generosity in spending countless hours in preparing a terrific abundance of great food, with and for others, in great love. There is no greater enthusiasm nor larger hearts in this world than in my husband's family.

All people in the world today who enjoy food are indebted to the tireless efforts of countless cooks who have perfected deliciousness and then generously shared what they have learned. A great big thank you to all who continue to make the necessaries of eating to stay alive a joy. Being able to share this human experience with others is part of that which truly helps to make life worth living!

The Pure Pleasure of Eating

Too often, the success of a meal is judged by the fleeting entertainment of a flavorgasm. If any one element of a dining experience is not the epitome of deliciousness, the search continues, to find The Ultimate Recipe, the one which, when added to the menu, will make diners swoon.

Food must be more than palatable: it must be pleasing and delightful. Food must put a song in your gut, leave one refreshed and content. Great menus offer foods that, in combination, create complementary eating sensations. They naturally lead one to eat in quantities that are satisfying. They do not demand an overindulgence.

Rather, when planning meals, think in wholistic terms. The epitome of perfection in food is to nourish the body and promote health and happiness. The greatest foods are designed to leave one fulfilled without creating a yearning for more and yet more.

Keep Foods Fresh

Bread   Before covering for extended freshness, allow the bread to cool completely. If wrapping in an air-tight container, include a paper or cloth towel to absorb any moisture. If storing in a plastic bag, cut a little hole in the plastic, here and there, to allow moisture to continue to escape. Don't leave bread in a place where it will come into contact with heat or direct sunlight. And, fingerprints on bread grow mold.

Chocolate   Most breads, cookies, and muffins can be eaten soon out of the oven, but those with chocolate chips should be allowed to cool longer before eating, enough so that you don't burn your mouth on the molten chocolate, which can remain quite hot even after the cookie itself has somewhat cooled to the touch.

Icing   Though a treat is served with icing, the icing is to be eaten, or not, as to one's individual tastes. Use your fork to apply as much or as little as you prefer to each bite and feel free to leave the rest on the plate. Consider icing as a condiment. After eating one's French fries, there is no need to eat up the rest of the leftover ketchup. So it is, with icing. You may leave some or all on the plate for Miss Manners and she will not be offended, but also, she will not be surprised if you do choose to eat it all.

Pies   Allow a pie to cool completely after baking. If it won't be eaten within a day or two, cover with plastic wrap before refrigerating to limit flavors and odors from other foods. To keep the plastic from sticking to the pie, stick in a few toothpicks here and there to hold the wrap up off the surface.

Delicious Dining

In general, whole milk and real sugar make food taste better and give a more satisfying mouthfeel than low-fat dairy products or artificial sweeteners. We want to eat a wide variety of nutritious, delicious foods and not too much of any one thing. But, if a food is terrific, you might feel the desire to keep eating more and more.

The dining experience should be joyful and gratifying, but sensibly limited and not laden with guilt or burdened with self-denial. That said, it is true that some foods are so yummy that it is very hard to say to yourself, "Stop! I've had enough!" even when you are trying to limit calories or know you need to leave room for more nutritious food.

Some of the recipes in this book may be off-limits to those watching their weight or advised by their doctors. Unfortunately for some of us, it is already too late to safely enjoy some of these recipes at all. But tailoring any of these recipes to make them suit individual constraints might affect consistency or flavor. Rather, select tasty alternatives which fit your nutritional goals.

Everyone should have the right to feel safe in their own home, safe even from the temptation to overeat. No one should be home alone with 3,000 calories of scrumptious irresistibility calling to them from the kitchen counter. Portions can be controlled by sharing good foods with others. Want to eat a slice of cake or a cookie? Have a baking party and designate a recipient willing to take home leftovers.

Do not hesitate to make any of these recipes, wondering what you will do with the mistakes. I give you permission to throw away whatever you realize you shouldn't eat—even if it is fresh out of the oven.

It's your body, your life. In later years, you may savor the memories of having once inhaled the aroma of the very best.

Maintain Your Wok

You will find out that it is work to make great food. Learn, and practice. Like keeping a wok well-seasoned, it is worth the time and trouble it takes to perfect cooking techniques. But, like writing poetry, creating food is complicated. It is not always so easy to figure out the best methods that will lead to satisfying solutions. Exploring ways to keep yourself alive and healthy is a process that requires your full attention and the use of your whole brain.

These delicious recipes come with a caveat. Don't trust words on a page. Keep learning, to understand what works for you. Every human body is different.

Sometimes delicious food is junk food. I have tried to include all kinds of recipes. Some are both nourishing and taste terrific. But beware. Sometimes excellence in flavor leads one onto a pathway towards over-indulgence, a course that could result in self-destruction.

These foods are good, I believe. But, maybe, they're too good. If you think one might not be good for you, don't eat it.

How to Follow These Recipes

L earning the art of cooking involves getting a feel for how the ingredients should look, feel, taste, and smell as they come together, using various tools and techniques. This guide is meant to be a set of helpful hints, for those who are just learning to cook. Be consistent in your treatment of your ingredients and in the timing of your actions. Leave the rest of your life outside the kitchen door; keep a relaxed and happy attitude each time you create something delicious. Your cake won't forgive you if you beat the eggs extra hard when you are mad!

Add   To "add" ingredients, add the ingredients to the bowl in the order suggested. If no directions are given for mixing speed or how to mix the ingredients together, they may be gently mixed together with a spoon by hand.

Butter   To "butter" the baking pan before adding the muffin or cake batter, completely coat the entire interior surface of the muffin tin or cake pan with a thin layer of slightly softened butter. This prevents the batter from sticking to the pan when cooking, even as the cake rises to the top edge of the pan. To aid in spreading the butter evenly, I like to wrap around my fingers a clean bit of plastic wrap or use a piece of food-quality paper, such as that in which sticks of butter are packaged, and use it as sort of a brush, to "paint" the pan with butter.

Butter and flour   When the recipe instructs to "butter and flour" the pan, the idea is to make very sure that the bottom of the treat does not stick to the pan after baking, so that when you use a spatula or turn the pan upside down to remove the treat, the treat comes out in one piece. First, butter the pan, as described above. Next, add a tablespoon of flour to the pan, adding more flour as needed, and shake the pan side to side, tapping the edges, so that the butter becomes completely coated with a thin layer of flour. After the pan is buttered and floured, turn the pan upside-down and tap the pan to shake out the excess flour. If the treat is chocolate, cocoa powder can be used instead of white flour.

Coating Mix together the "coating" ingredients and set aside.

Combine Mix together the listed ingredients by adding them to a bowl and lightly stirring with a spoon, then set aside.

Cool A recipe will call for allowing treats to "cool" before being removed from the pan, to give them a chance to set, so they can be safely removed without falling apart. However, if left to cool too long, they may stick to the pan, in some cases becoming stuck fast as the caramelized sugar hardens, so the treat breaks apart when you take it out. It is important to learn how to recognize how a treat's consistency feels to the touch, to know when it is just the right time to take it out of the pan.

Cupcakes The batter for "cupcakes" is usually spooned into cupcake liners in a cupcake pan, because most cupcakes might stick to a pan, even if it is first buttered and floured. If cupcake liners are not available, just butter and flour the pan, but soon after baking, slide a knife in between the cupcake and the tin and pry it loose if it is sticking around the edges. Turn the pan upside down to shake out the cupcakes before the sugars have a chance to harden.

Doneness test Some recipes call for the use of a "doneness test," to determine if baked treats are done. Just in case the treats do need more baking time, keep both the oven and the treats as hot as possible while testing, by working quickly. If possible, just slide out the shelf containing the pan, test quickly, and slide it back in. If you need to take the pan out of the oven to do the test, take the pan out, put it on a heat-proof surface like a stovetop or on an oven mitt on a table or counter, shut the oven door, and then test. Repeat the bake and test cycle until the treat passes the doneness test, then remove from the oven. Doneness tests include the "finger press test," "knife test," and "toothpick test" or checking the color of the bottom of the treat.

Dry ingredients   The "dry ingredients" are the flour, salt, baking soda, and baking powder. When any combination of these are called for in a recipe in making a batter or dough, they should first be combined by mixing them together. If there are dry spices to be added to the dry ingredients, combine the spices first before adding them to the dry ingredients. If there are pieces of fruit, vegetables, or nuts to be added to a batter, these are often first mixed in with the combined dry ingredients, to coat them, just before the wet ingredients are then added to the bowl. This coating helps keep these pieces from sinking to the bottom, so gently mix in the wet ingredients without over stirring.

Finger press test   To do the "finger press test" for doneness, use one finger to gently press down on the center of the treat, and release quickly. If the depressed area springs right back up, the treat is done.

Grease   If a recipe says to "grease" rather than "butter" the baking pan before adding the batter, use vegetable oil or shortening. At higher temperatures, butter might burn.

Icing   It is important to wait until a treat is completely cool before "icing." Applied to a warm treat, some icings will melt and run, some might cook, and some that need to be refrigerated, like whipped cream, might spoil quickly. Add sprinkles immediately after icing, before the surface hardens, or they won't stick. If called for in a recipe, icing is not optional, even if you don't plan to eat it. Icing is a semi-hard barrier which helps to keep a baked treat fresh and flavorful and maintain its consistency. Icing prevents evaporation, keeps in moistness, and keeps out dampness. Icing helps to preserve flavor by keeping out air, which may contain other flavors and odors.

Knife test   The "knife test" for doneness involves taking a butter knife and sticking the blade straight down into the thickest part of the center of the treat, and then pulling it out again immediately. If the treat is not done, some of the batter or pie filling may cling to the knife.

Layer To "layer" ingredients, spread each layer flat and out to the edges of the pan. Then add the next layer.

Loosen Shortly after baking, slide a butter knife gently around the edge of the pan, to loosen the treat from the sides. Remove from the pan after cooling for a short time, so the treat has a chance to hold together, but before the sugars and fats have a chance to cool and making it more likely that the treat would stick to the pan.

Mix To "mix" ingredients, put them all in a large bowl at once and gently stir them together gently, just enough to combine thoroughly, but not vigorously enough to add air bubbles to the mixture, as happens in beating eggs or whipping cream. When combining "dry ingredients" and "wet ingredients," I find it easier to first combine the dry ingredients, then combine the wet ingredients, and finally add the dry ingredients to the bowl containing the wet ingredients.

Muffins "Muffins" can be made in a muffin tin or a mini-muffin tin, which requires less baking time. Grease the tin with butter, do not use cupcake liners. The dry ingredients are added to the wet ingredients and stirred until just combined.

Remove After baking, allow the treat to cool shortly, to set. Loosen from the pan. Then "remove" cakes, cupcakes, loaves, and breads from the pan by turning the pan upside down, shaking gently, if necessary. If a cake is not holding together, it may come out in separate pieces. Pieces that are still stuck to the bottom of the can pan may be loosened with a butter knife or spatula and picked up. The cake may then be pieced back together on the cake plate, "glued" back together with icing, if necessary. Cookies may be removed shortly after baking. Give cookies a minute or so to set first, so they hold together, and then gently pry them off the pan with a spatula. Place cookies on flattened brown paper bags, brown paper, parchment paper, absorbent paper plates, paper towels, or cotton dish towels, to absorb fats and moisture as they cool. If sticky, move them around occasionally until fully cooled, to prevent sticking to the paper.

Spices All the powdered spices should be mixed together before being added.

Toothpick test The "toothpick test" for doneness involves taking a single toothpick and sticking it all the way down into the thickest part of the center of the treat, and then pulling it out again immediately. If the treat is not done, some of the batter or pie filling may cling to the toothpick.

Topping Mix together the topping ingredients and set aside. Spread evenly over top of treat just before baking.

Wet Ingredients The wet ingredients should be combined in order, before adding the dry ingredients. Cream the butter until fluffy. Add sugar, and cream again until light and fluffy. Add the rest of the wet ingredients and mix until well combined. Note: granulated cane sugar is considered a "wet" ingredient.

Ingredients

Foundations for a Healthful Morsel

Fitness starts with good nutrition, the foundation for a healthy body which gives us the energy to move and think and keep well. Our choices in the supermarket are vastly different than they were fifty years ago, so why should we learn to prepare food, to "cook" as our parents did? Great cooking in that fashion leads to overindulgence in deliciousness, leading to obesity and disability; not to mention that it is an inefficient use of a person's time, and that person is more often a woman, whose time is too often not seen as valuable anyway. This has to change.

Parents are often too busy or too uninformed to lead by good example. Children need to learn how to make better food selections to nourish themselves, to avoid processed foods, to resist food as entertainment, and to share food around the globe and not just with family at the dinner table of each individual household. The economics of feeding a planet full of busy people indicates that efficiency in production is required to yield nutritious foods requiring little preparation time.

The over-processing of actual plants into "food" with little to no nutritional value leads to even the wealthy becoming malnourished. The lack of nutritious food leads to poor brain development, physical and psychological disabilities, and eventually to personal incompetence and political instability. The story is that Rome was brought down by toxic lead, a "new-and-improved" material that unfortunately made its way into the food chain, poisoning its residents. Our modern civilization could be brought down by malnutrition caused by innovation in food production unmindful of the need for proper nourishment combined with the successful marketing of non-nutritious substitutes for real food.

Along with studying how to improve flavors, stabilize consistency, and prolong shelf-life, "food science" should concentrate on how to retain nutrients and get real nourishment to everyone's table quickly.

We need to stop asking the food industry to entertain our palettes. We can find other ways to pamper ourselves. We want to teach our kids to demand nutritious, natural foods.

Select the Best Ingredients

Use the freshest ingredients! In this section, the ingredients named in these recipes are described in more detail. Brand names, when noted, are selected for consistency in flavor, texture, and nutritional content and/or economic value. Given continual innovations in the food production and processing industries, the quality, nutritional value, and availability of ingredients will continue to change, so this list may become outdated at any time. At least it is preserved here for the history books. An experienced cook may know whether a different ingredient or brand may be substituted if what's called for in a recipe is unavailable. This guide is for those who are unfamiliar with an ingredient or those who are on a budget but still want tasty results.

Alcohol Watching the football game on the big screen with the brothers-in-law: beer. My favorites, Molson Golden Ale and Corona Extra with a slice of lime. Cooking wine for salad dressing, sushi rolls, or stew—dry sherry, rice wine, and burgundy, respectively. For pre-dinner conversation or to treat a lingering cough: blackberry brandy. White wine goes with crab; red wine with red pasta sauce. Sterling Cabernet Sauvignon anytime. To add to after-dinner coffee: Kaluha, Bailey's Irish Creme; creme de cacao; or cognac. On days when it rained and the ice-cream truck didn't come, my great-aunt used to drizzle creme de menthe on vanilla ice cream for our dessert at sleepovers in her first-floor apartment with the iron bars on the windows. After dinner, my Irish grandfather and uncle each had shots of whiskey. So did the gang at the high school where I grew up, but they didn't wait until dinner. At pool parties in the neighborhood, they served the grownups Southern Comfort; pre-teens made their own "Tequila Sunrises"; those responsible for driving home had gin. For breakfast, a hair of the dog that bit you might be vodka in OJ, a splash of champagne. Try AA.

Apples For baking: Granny Smith, Rome. For eating: Gala, Red Delicious,Yellow Delicious. Applesauce: Mott's Natural.

Asparagus Fresh. Hold a spear, one end in each hand, and fold the spear in half. This will snap off the tough end at its natural breaking point. Keep the end with the flowerets and discard the thicker hard stem.

Avocado Fresh. Allow it to ripen. Peel and pit, then slice or gently mash with fork.

Baked beans Canned, do not drain. Preferred flavor has bacon and brown sugar or molasses. Add minced onion, ketchup, molasses, bits of cooked bacon, a little mustard.

Baking mix "Bisquick." Use whole milk and follow recipe.

Baking powder "Davis."

Baking soda "Arm & Hammer."

Banana "Chiquita." For banana bread, select large bananas or the equivalent measure in smaller or larger bananas. Choose bananas which are overripe, to the point where you probably don't want to eat them anymore, but not yet mushy. Freshly bruised areas are ok, but avoid older bruised areas where the flavor may have turned. Peel, then gently mash with a fork on a plate. Maintain one-third of the banana as 1/4-inch chunks, and fully press the rest into slabs of mashed banana with the tines of the fork, separating each flattened bit from the next, so they stir easily into the recipe without vigorous mixing.

Barley Any brand is fine. Dried.

Beans, lentils, or split peas; for soup or stew or salad Any brand is fine. Use in any combination of any of these varieties of bean: black beans, chick peas (garbanzo beans), kidney beans, pink beans. For canned beans: pour off and discard the liquid, empty the can and save the beans for use in the recipe, discard the can with the sediment at the bottom of the can. For dried beans, split peas, or lentils: rinse, carefully pick over and remove any extraneous material. Add with water to cover and bring to a boil in a pot, simmer ten minutes, remove from heat, soak at least three hours or overnight in refrigerator. Add more water and boil to desired tenderness, discard excess liquid.

Bell pepper Fresh; any combination of green, red, orange, and yellow bell peppers. Slice open lengthwise, cut out stem and discard, discard seeds, cut out tough white membranes and discard. For frozen: Any brand is fine, plain, no added ingredients, cut in any style.

Black beans "Goya." Canned. Drain.

Blueberries Any brand is fine. Frozen. Thaw, rinse, drain. Use fresh blueberries, if available and reasonably priced.

Broccoli Fresh, crowns. Cut into 1-inch bits. For recipes that are stewed or cooked a long time, the broccoli stems may be used, pared to remove the 1/16-inch tough outer shell, and sliced into 1/8-inch slices.

Brown sugar "Domino." Dark brown sugar.

Butter "Land O'Lakes." Salted. Room temperature.

Cabbage Fresh. Cut out tough core at base end and discard.

Cantaloupe Fresh. Allow to ripen, pare, remove seeds and seed membranes, cut off tough ends, cut into 1-in chunks. For fancy presentation: cut into 1/2-inch arcs.

Carrot Fresh. Pare. Cut off tough ends.

Cashews "Planter's." Shelled, salted.

Cheddar Cheese In my local ShopRite, I buy "NY Cheddar." Sharp.

Cheese American cheese: "Kraft." Yellow singles.

Chick peas "Goya." Canned. Drain.

Chilis Any brand is fine. Green, canned, diced. Drain, if lots of liquid; otherwise, use with liquid.

Chocolate chips "Nestle's." Semi-sweet morsels.

Chocolate packets "Nestle's." Pre-melted chocolate in a packet. If not available, use 1 oz "Bakers" semi-sweet chocolate, melted and cooled to room temperature.

Chocolate pudding "Royal." Chocolate pudding packets, prepared according to package directions.

Chocolate syrup "Hershey's." Dark chocolate syrup.

Cocoa powder "Hershey's."

Confectioner's sugar "Domino."

Corn starch "Argo."

Cottage cheese "Breakstone." Milkfat 4%.

Cranberry sauce "Ocean Spray." Whole berry cranberry sauce. For use as a condiment: "Ocean Spray" cranberry-orange sauce.

Cream cheese "Philadelphia." Original.

Cucumber Fresh. Do not pare. Cut off tough ends.

Dairy Unless recipe specifies differently, all dairy products are those made with whole milk.

Eggs "Eggland's Best." Extra-large.

Flour "Hecker's" or "King Arthur." Unbleached, white, bread flour.

French fried onions "French's." In plastic-coated paper box.

Garlic Fresh. Remove papery outer peel, cut off hard stem end, slice cloves lengthwise into 1/16" strips.

Gelatin "Jell-O." With sugar. Prepare according to package directions.

Green beans Any brand is fine. Frozen, plain, no added ingredients, French-cut. For canned: "Del Monte," drained, not French-cut. For fresh: cut off tough ends and discard, cut into 2-inch bits.

Green olives Any brand is fine. Green olives stuffed with pimiento. Drain.

Heavy cream Any brand is fine.

Honey "Golden Blossom" or fresh local honey. Clover honey.

Ice cream "Breyer's": chocolate, vanilla, strawberry, peach, black cherry chocolate, vanilla fudge swirl, black raspberry swirl. "Turkey Hill": green chocolate chip mint. "Starbucks": Java Chip. "Dove Bars": chocolate ice cream dipped in dark chocolate. "Luigi's Ice": lemon ice. "ShopRite": ice cream sandwiches, orange or rainbow sherbet. "Friendly's": butter pecan, rocky road.

Iceberg lettuce Fresh. Cut out tough core at base end and discard.

Jalapeño Any brand is fine. Canned, sliced in rounds. Drain. A recipe may also call for minced jalapeño.

Jam "Welch's": grape jam. "Smucker's": strawberry, apricot, peach, raspberry, seedless raspberry, and black raspberry jams.

Jelly "Welch's": grape jelly. Any brand is fine for red currant jelly.

Kidney beans Any brand is fine. Canned, dark red. Drain.

Lemon juice "ReaLemon." Bottled. Fresh-squeezed is better.

Lentils Any brand is fine. Dried. Rinse. Carefully pick over and remove any extraneous material.

Lettuce Fresh. Romaine. Remove tough white center from greens and discard. Tear into 2-inch bits. Watch the news for the latest warnings about salmonella.

Lima beans Any brand is fine. Frozen, no added ingredients.

Lime juice "ReaLime." Bottled. Fresh-squeezed is better. Use Key Lime lime juice for Key Lime Pie.

Mandarin oranges Any brand is fine. Canned. Drain.

Marmalade "Smucker's": orange marmalade.

Milk Fresh, whole milk. If fresh milk is not available, "Parmalat" boxed milk may be used, but only in some recipes.

Mini chocolate chips "Nestle's." Mini semi-sweet morsels.

Molasses "Grandma's." Dark molasses, also known as black-strap molasses.

Mustard "Gulden's." Spicy brown.

Nori Any brand is fine. Dark green, flat, paper-thin, squares of seaweed; approximately 10"x10", or any size.

Oatmeal "Quaker." Plain, dry oatmeal. Not steel-cut nor instant nor flavored oatmeal.

Oil Any brand is fine. Vegetable oil made from corn, canola, soybean, or peanut. Different vegetable oils burn at different temperatures; don't use olive oil for frying or stir-frying.

Olive oil Any good brand is fine. Extra-virgin olive oil has the most flavor.

Olives Any brand is fine. Black olives, canned, small, pitted, sliced. Drain. For whole olives, use the largest size.

Onion Fresh. Yellow. Pare, cut out tough core at top and discard; slice into 1/8" x 2" strips, unless recipe describes a different cut. May use frozen onions in soups, stews, and stir-fry, but not in fresh salads.

Orange juice "Tropicana Pure Premium." Original. No pulp.

Peanut butter "Skippy." Super Chunk. "Jiff": Creamy.

Peanuts "Planter's." Shelled, salted.

Peas Any brand is fine. Frozen, no added ingredients, any size. Use fresh peas if available: remove from outer pod shell, boil in water until tender, drain.

Pepper Any brand is fine. Black pepper, ground.

Peppers Fresh: bell pepper. Canned: chili, jalapeno. Pickled in jar: banana peppers, ghost peppers.

Pickle relish "Heinz." India Relish.

Pickles "Vlasic." Dill, sweet gherkins, hamburger slices.

Pineapple "Dole." Canned, in heavy syrup. Drain. For fresh: "Dole," pare, core, cut into 1-inch chunks.

Pink beans "Goya." Canned. Drain.

Pizza sauce "Pizza Quick."

Plastic I stopped buying fast-food salads after discovering, one too many time, large shards of plastic at the bottom

Raisins "Sun-Maid."

Rice vinegar Any brand is fine.

Rice wine vinegar Any brand is fine.

Salsa "Tostitos." Habenero. Chunky, hot.

Salt "Diamond Crystal." Iodized salt.

Sardines "Season." Packed in oil.

Shortening "Crisco."

Sour cream "Breakstone." Original.

Soy sauce Mushroom soy sauce, which comes in a large square plastic jug from the Chinese grocery store on Route 27 in Edison, NJ. This is thicker, and not the same as grocery store brand soy sauce or the packets from Chinese take-out restaurants.

Spaghetti "Ronzoni." No. 10 spaghetti, or any premium brand spaghetti of the same diameter or thickness. I prefer whole wheat or spinach pasta and my husband and kids prefer the plain spaghetti made by Ronzoni. I prefer No. 10-sized spaghetti, my husband prefers No. 11, my youngest daughter prefers bow-tie pasta – and we are all spoiled rotten. Ronzoni No. 10 spaghetti is our compromise, although occasionally we do take the trouble to be short-order cooks and give every member of the family the type of pasta they prefer. Life is too short to not eat what you prefer, at least some of the time.

Spaghetti sauce "Prego." Chunky Garden Combo, Three-Cheese, Fresh Mushroom, and Tomato and Garlic are my favorites. My eldest son prefers Prego Traditional, which he heats in a little bowl in the microwave and dips French bread into.

Spices "McCormick." Dried, in glass bottles. Organic, if available.

Split peas Any brand is fine. Dried. Rinse, carefully pick over and remove any extraneous material.

Strawberries Fresh. In season, pick the same day, rinse well. Remove stem. Unless recipe calls for whole strawberries, remove most of the white core, slice. Any frozen brand is fine.

Sugar Any brand is fine. Granulated white sugar.

Taco seasoning mix "Ortega." Original.

Taco sauce "Ortega." Medium.

Taco shells "Ortega." Yellow.

Tomato For canned: "Redpack," plum tomatoes or crushed with puree, do not drain. For fresh: "Ugly Ripe." For fresh plum tomato: any brand is fine.

Tomato paste "Hunt's." Canned. Italian Seasonings.

Tomato puree "Redpack." Canned.

Tortilla Any brand is fine. Flour tortillas, unless recipe calls for corn tortillas.

Tortilla chip "Tostitos." Restaurant style.

Tuna "Starkist." Packed in water. Drain. Flake with fork. Larger cans seem to have better quality fish.

Vanilla "McCormick." Pure vanilla extract.

Vegetable juice "V-8." Original or Extra Spicy.

Vinegar Any brand is fine. White vinegar.

Vitamins "One-a-Day Gummies" are tasty.

Walnuts "Diamond Walnut." Shelled. In pieces, not whole.

Water Tap water. Since tap water may contain important minerals, avoid water filtered by a water softener. Since tap water contains whatever seeps into the local aquifer, prepare to experience the effects of mind-altering medications in areas where they are frequently prescribed. Don't dispose of any unused medications by flushing them down the toilet.

Watermelon Fresh. Chill immediately after purchase. Pare, cut off white pith, cut into 1-inch chunks, discard seeds. Eat immediately after cutting.

Wheat cereal "Cream of Wheat." Original 10-Minute Cream of Wheat, not flavored, nor instant, nor 5-minute.

Wheat germ "Kretchmer's." Toasted, plain, in glass jar. Keep refrigerated, use within three months of opening.

White sauce Make it fresh, see recipe "White Sauce."

List of Commmon Ingredients and Preferred Brands

If a preferred brand is listed, I have found it to be consistently better in some way. Suitability for use in a recipe may not differ significantly by brand, but a differing manufacturing process may lead to differences in taste or consistency.

alcohol
   creme de menthe
   (Bailey's Irish Creme)
   beer (Molson Golden Ale, Corona Extra)
   blackberry brandy
   brandy
   burgundy
   cognac
   cooking wine, dry sherry
   creme de cacao
   gin
   (Kaluha)
   sake
   (Southern Comfort)
   tequila
   vodka
   whiskey
   wine, red (Sterling Cabernet Sauvignon)
   wine, rice
   wine, sherry
   wine, white
apples
   applesauce (Motts, Natural)
   baking (Granny Smith, Rome)
   eating (Fuji, Gala, Red Delicious,Yellow Delicious)
beans, dried peas, and legumes
   3-bean salad
   barley
   black beansIngredient   page
   chick peas

garbanzo beans

beans, dried peas, and legumes (cont.)

    kidney beans
    lentils
    pink beans
    soy beans
    soy milk
    split peas

beef

    beef stew
    corned beef
    filet mignon
    hamburger
    sirloin steak

bread and rolls

    bagels
    biscuit mix (Bisquick)
    bread crumbs (4C, seasoned)
    bread cubes (Pepperidge Farm)
    crepes
    croutons
    English muffins (Thomas's)
    French baguette
    French bread
    fry bread
    hamburger rolls (Pepperidge Farm, seeded)
    hot dog rolls (Pepperidge Farm, top-sliced)
    Italian bread
    kaiser rolls
    long bread
    potato rolls
    portuguese rolls
    pumpernickel bread
    rye bread
    scallion pancakes
    sourdough bread
    sourdough starter
    stuffing mix (Pepperidge Farm)
    sub rolls

tortillas, soft, corn
tortillas, soft, flour
waffles
wheat (Dave's Killer Bread)
whole wheat bread
yeast
cake, pie, and pastry
    apple turnover
    biscotti
    icing
    pumpkin, canned
    pumpkin pie mix, canned
    scones
    sponge cake
candy
    almonds, sugared
    (Baby Ruth)
    (Butterfinger)
    butterscotch
    candy canes
    caramels
    dark chocolates (Dove)
    Easter bunny (Dove)
    gum drops
    jelly beans (Starburst)
    licorice, black
    licorice, red (Twizzlers)
    (Life-Savers)
    marshmallows, larger or mini (Kraft)
    (Mary Janes)
    (M&Ms)
    molasses chew, dark chocolate (Billy's Candies)
    non-pareils
    peppermints
    (Raisinets)
    milk chocolate bar with almonds (Hershey's)
    sprinkles
    (Skittles)
    (Toblerone)

cereal
  bran (All-Bran)
  (Cheerios)
  (Honey-Nut Cheerios)
  oatmeal (Quaker, original)
  (Rice Krispies)
  (Shredded Wheat, bite-sized mini wheats)
  (Wheat Chex, original)
  (Wheateena)
cheese
  American cheese (Kraft, yellow singles)
  bleu cheese
  Brie cheese (President's)
  cheddar, sharp, yellow, New York
  cheddar jack cheese
  colby cheese
  colby jack
  cream cheese (Philadelphia)
  Edam cheese
  feta cheese
  ghost pepper
  goat cheese
  Gouda cheese
  mozzarella
  Parmesan/Romano
  string cheese
  Swiss cheese
chicken
  chicken boneless breast (Purdue)
  chicken boneless breast (Purdue)
  chicken breast (Purdue)
  chicken broth
  chicken nuggets
  cranberry chicken salad (Hayek's)
  chicken cutlets
  chicken gravy
  chicken legs (Purdue)
  chicken thighs (Purdue)
  chicken wings (Purdue Wingettes)

chocolate
  baking chocolate (Baker's)
  cocoa powder (Hershey's)
  semi-sweet chocolate morsels (Nestle's)
  semi-sweet chocolate packets (Nestle's)
  syrup, dark chocolate (Hershey's)
cookies, crackers, chips, and pretzels
  graham crackers (Nabisco)
  graham crackers, chocolate covered
  marzipan
  Milanos (Pepperidge Farm)
  potato chips (Lay's)
  pretzels
  pretzels, dark chocolate covered (Billy's Candies)
  saltines (Nabisco)
  (Stoned Wheat, mini)
  tortilla chips (Tostitos)
  (Wheat Thins, original)
  vanilla wafers
dried fruits
  apricots
  cherries
  cranberries
  dates
  figs
  golden raisins
  mango
  prunes (Sunsweet)
  raisins
eggs
  1,000-year-old eggs
  egg white
  egg yolk
  pickled eggs
  red beet eggs
  scrambled eggs
fish
  clams
  cod

crab cakes, hot and spicy (ShopRite)
sticks
flounder
fried clams
herring (Vita, with onions in wine sauce)
lobster
mussels
oysters
salmon
salt fish
sardines (Season)
seasoning, lobster boil
shrimp
tuna, packed in water (Starkist)
flour and leavening
bread flour (King Arthur's, Hecker's)
corn meal
cream of tartar
graham cracker crumbs
poolish
rice
rye
self-rising
sourdough starter
soy
wheat germ (Kretchmer's' toasted)
wheat gluten
white
whole wheat
yeast
fruits
apricots
bananas
blackberries
blueberries
cantaloupe
cherries
cherry pie filling
coconut flakes

coconut, shredded
coconuts
cranberries
cranberry sauce, whole berry (Ocean Spray)
cranberry sauce
grapefruits
grapes, green, seedless
key limes
lemon ice
lemon peel
lemon sauce
lemon zest
lemons
lima beans
lime zest
limes
Mandarin oranges
mango
Maraschino cherries
orange zest
oranges
peaches
pears
pineapple chunks (Dole)
pineapple slices (Dole)
pineapple tidbits (Dole)
plums
raspberries
sherbet
starfruit
strawberries
watermelon
jam and jelly
apricot jam
black currant jelly
black raspberry jam
grape jam
grape jelly
guava jelly

mint jelly
orange mamalade
peach jam
raspberry jam, with seeds
red currant jelly
strawberry jam, seedless
juice
    apple (Motts Natural)
    (Clamato)
    cranberry grape (Ocean Spray)
    grape (Welch's)
    grapefruit, pink (Tropicana)
    guanabana (Goya)
    guava
    Key Lime
    lemon (ReaLemon)
    mango (Goya)
    orange (Tropicana original, no pulp)
    pear
    pineapple grapefruit
    pineapple
    pineapple orange
    tomato
    vegetable (V-8 Spicy Hot)
lamb
    lamb chop
    leg of lamb
lettuces and green vegetables
    alfalfa sprouts
    artichoke
    artichoke hearts
    asparagus
    avocado
    bean sprouts
    beans, green, French cut
    bell peppers
    bibb lettuce
    Boston lettuce
    broccoli

cabbage
celeriac
celery
chives
cucumbers
iceberg lettuce
kale
kohlrabi
leek
napa cabbage
nori
peas, green
red cabbage
red lettuce
Romaine lettuce
scallions
snow peas
spinach
Swiss chard
meatloaf mix
 ground beef, lamb, and pork
meats, processed
 bacon
 bacon, fake (Bacos)
 bologna
 ham
 ham, canned (Spam)
 hot dogs
 kielbasi
milk products
 (see: cheese, puddings and custard, yogurt)
 butter, salted (Land O'Lakes)
 butter, unsalted (Land O'Lakes)
 buttermilk
 buttermilk powder
 cream cheese (Philadelphia, original)
 cream, heavy
 evaporated milk
 half and half

ice cream (Breyer's)
ice cream bar, chocolate, chocolate dipped (Dove)
milk, whole milk
non-fat dry milk
whipped cream (Redi-Whip, original)
sour cream, original (Breakstone's)
sweetened condensed milk
yogurt, Stoneyfield whole milk strawberry, quart
mushrooms
  mushrooms, white
nuts and seeds
  almonds
  Brazil nuts
  caraway seeds
  cashews
  hazelnuts
  macademia nuts
  peanut butter (Jiff, Creamy)
  peanut butter (Skippy, Super Chunk)
  peanuts (Planters)
  pecans
  pistachios
  poppy seeds
  sesame seeds
  sunflower seeds
  walnuts
oils, shortenings, and vinegars
  balsamic vinegar
  ghee
  olive oil
  red wine vinegar
  rice wine vinegar
  sesame oil
  shortening (Crisco)
  vegetable oils: cannola, peanut, soybean
  white vinegar
olives
  black
  green, with pimiento

onions, garlic, ginger, radishes
    daikon radish
    French fried onions
    garlic
    ginger root
    onion flakes
    onion powder
    onion rings
    onion salt
    radishes
    Vidalia onions
pasta and noodles
    bow tie macaroni
    elbow macaroni
    homestyle noodles (Pennsylvania Dutch)
    lasagna noodles
    linguine noodles
    orzo pasta
    pasta shells
    rotini pasta
    spaghetti noodles
    wagon wheel pasta
peppers, salt and pepper
    banana peppers
    bell peppers
    black pepper
    cayenne pepper
    chili paste
    chili peppers
    chili powder
    jalapeno peppers
    kosher salt
    peppercorns
    red pepper flakes
    red pepper sauce
    salt, iodized, Diamond Crystal
    white pepper
pickles
    dill pickles

gherkins
India relish
mixed pickles
pickled cabbage
picked Chinese vegetable
pickled mustard greens
pickled onions
pickled red beets
pork
   ham steak
   hot sausage
   pork chops
   pork loin
   pork roll (Taylor Ham)
   sweet Italian sausage
potatoes, corn, beets, root vegetables, eggplant, squash
   carrots
   creamed corn
   eggplant
   French fries
   hash browns
   latkes
   potato pancakes
   red beets
   squash: acorn, butternut, spaghetti, yellow, zucchini
   sweet potatoes
   tater tots
   turnips
   yams
pudding and custard
   chocolate pudding (Royal)
   custard
   custard sauce
   flan
   gelatin
   Jell-O (black cherry, lemon, lime)
   lemon curd
   lemon pudding
   rennet custard

tapioca
tapioca pudding
vanilla pudding
rice
basmati
brown rice
fried rice
white rice
salad dressing and condiments
(A-1 Steak Sauce)
barbecue sauce (Kraft)
bleu cheese dressing
duck sauce
French dressing
honey mustard
Italian dressing
ketchup (Heinz, organic)
(Marie's Coleslaw Dressing)
(Marie's Raspberry Vinaigrette)
mayonnaise (Hellman's)
(Miracle Whip)
Russian dressing
tartar sauce
soda and non-alcoholic drinks
birch beer
cocoa
coffee
cola (Coca Cola, in glass bottles)
cream soda
ginger ale
lemon-lime soda (7-Up)
orange soda
tea
water
soup, broth, boullion, and gravy
alphabet soup (Campbell's)
beef broth
beef gravy
boullion, chicken

chicken broth
chicken gravy
Cream of Celery Soup (Campbell's)
Cream of Chicken Soup (Campbell's)
Cream of Mushroom Soup (Campbell's)
mushroom gravy
tomato (Campbell's)
turkey gravy
vegetable (Progresso)
spaghetti
(see: pasta, tomato sauce)
spices, flavoring, thickeners
(Adobe) seasonings
almond extract
apple pie spice
basil
bay leaf
black bean paste
blackening spice
Cajun blackening spice
Cajun seasoning
celery seeds
cinnamon
cinnamon hearts
cloves
corn starch
crystallized ginger
crystallized sugar
cumin
dijon mustard
dill
dry mustard
fish sauce
garlic powder
garlic salt
ginger powder
ginger root
hoisin sauce
horseradish

hot sauce
Italian seasoning
lemon extract
mushroom soy sauce
mustard
nutmeg
orange extract
oregano
oyster sauce
paprika
parsley
parsley flakes
poultry seasoning
pumpkin pie spice
rosemary
sage
soy sauce
teriyaki sauce
thyme
tumeric powder
vanilla bean
vanilla extract, pure
Worcestershire sauce
sugar and sweeteners
    brown, dark and light
    colored sprinkles
    confectioner's
    corn syrup, dark and light (Karo)
    honey (Golden Blossom, clover)
    maple syrup
    molasses, blackstrap molasses (Grandma's)
    raw sugar
    simple syrup
    sugar cane
    superfine sugar
    vanilla sugar
tacos
    taco mix (Ortega)
    taco sauce (Ortega)

taco seasoning (Ortega)
taco shells, yellow (Ortega)
tofu
    hard tofu
    pressed tofu
    silken tofu
    soft tofu
tomatoes
    crushed, diced, or whole tomatoes (Redpack)
    fresh tomatoes (Ugli Ripe)
    pizza sauce (Pizza Quick)
    plum tomatoes (Redpack)
    salsa, habanero (Tostitos)
    sloppy joe sauce (Manwich)
    spaghetti sauce (Prego)
    tomato paste (Contadina)
    tomato puree (Redpack)
    tomato sauce (Redpack)
    pizza sauce (Pizza Quick)
turkey
    turkey breast
    turkey drumstick
    turkey gravy
    tv dinners, turkey (Hungry Man)
vanilla
    (see: pudding and custard)
    vanilla bean
    vanilla extract
    vanilla ice cream
    vanilla sugar
veal
    veal patty

FEEDING KIDS

Nurse Your Baby

Mother

   1 mother

Baby

   1 baby

World

   1 world

- Fall in love with your baby.
- Nurse your baby.

I came to understand that nursing is more than just a liquid transfer from mother to infant.

I believe that my maintaining the nursing relationship for the first three years of life is what was best for us both, mother and baby.

I discovered that nursing is a relationship that is natural and rewarding and, just as it is with any other meaningful human relationship, it has its challenges, but it is worth it to work hard to establish and maintain a successful nursing relationship.

I got help to overcome problems that interfered with nursing. Especially helpful were support groups where I met in person with other local nursing mothers and babies. Despite the rumors I heard that some individual members might tend to be fanatics, I joined the La Leche League, a group of nursing mothers, and I continue to support them financially. I appreciate now that people are people, no matter which organization they join.

If you find that your local group of nursing mothers offers no real support, BE the local group. You can be the one to support other nursing mothers and babies.

I avoided all machines and technology that supposedly "help" with nursing. I just nursed my baby. The act of baby/mother contact creates the milk and helps it flow.

- Listen to your baby. Learn from your baby. Teach your baby. Love your baby and let your baby love you. Be a part of each other's worlds.
- Take care of the mother, so she can nurse the baby.

Mothers of twins and triplets: I nursed my four children, including a set of twins, for almost three years each.

- Read about nursing. Read more about nursing. Learn all you can about nursing.
- If your nursing relationship is broken, mend it. If it has run into interference and is stopped, don't hesitate to restart it as soon as you are able. Keep trying.
- To the nursing couple: do not let the world come between the two of you.
- To the nursing mother: only you can make this happen. Make it happen, for you both.
- Enjoy your nursing relationship while it lasts. Remember and treasure it always.
- Don't wean until you both are ready.
- Encourage other mothers to develop and maintain nursing relationships with their babies. Help to educate them. Share your own experiences, especially with your own children, both daughters and sons.

Life. Enjoy.

Nourish Your Child

Parent

    you

Child

    your child

Food

    nourishing foods, often, and enough

When your child is born, see recipe "Nurse Your Baby."

Babies should only eat food that is nourishing and safe.

Prepare baby foods yourself using real ingredients that you recognize as products of nature that are closest to their natural form, not overly processed. When in doubt, choose foods recommended in the recipe "Anti-Acne Diet."

Teach your child to try foods with unfamiliar tastes.

Allow your child to eat right away when hungry so they can avoid the habit of eating when not hungry just to stave off hunger pangs.

As your child grows, bring your child with you into the food selection and preparation process. Educate about nutrition, health, fitness, and happiness. Emphasize the importance of nourishing the brain, rather than, or even at the expense of, coddling the tongue.

Teach your child that it is dangerous to use food as a source of entertainment or in self-medication.

Avoid giving foods that induce flavorgasms, which encourages overeating.

Teach your child that health and wellness through food is both an art and an area of scientific exploration, not a given set of approved grocery products and popular recipes and foods pre-packaged for convenience.

Keep abreast of the latest research, but learn to evaluate it rationally. Study health, nutrition, and chemistry.

When in doubt about a particular food, ask yourself, "Did my great-grandparents eat this?" If the answer is no, then most likely it is overprocessed and better to avoid. Try to find out what your great-grandparents did eat that nourished them well, and follow their example. Remember they most likely led a less sedentary lifestyle and ate more calories while maintaining a healthy weight. In adjusting caloric intake to meet today's reduction in physical energy output, it is important to guarantee dense nutritional value in every mouthful.

Anti-Acne Diet

How to Follow the Anti-Acne Diet

I AM NOT A DOCTOR!

First, for a complete diagnosis of any skin condition or to treat an active infection, please begin by seeking medical attention.

Do not follow this diet against medical advice!

The condition of acne, which may cause pain, inflammation, infection, scarring, and psychological and social discomfort, may either complicate or enhance the body's defense response against disease and other problems faced by humans. Who knows for sure whether acne is harmful or helpful?

We say "acne" like it is a bad thing, but we do not really know. It would be interesting to find out later that acne might actually be good for you, possibly because it stimulates the immune system. Maybe it's a positive because it helps young people maintain a wider social distance from others, protecting them from communicable diseases, early pregnancy, or unwanted sexual attention they may not be ready for. Maybe in washing the skin more frequently with soap and water to try to fight the acne, the person is better protected against other kinds of pathogens which might now be washed away. Maybe having such a skin condition that negatively affects one's satisfaction with one's appearance is key to developing a depth of compassion for others, because it introduces young people to a personal experience of their own suffering. This might have a profound positive affect on the entire population.

Maybe being a poet helps me to keep an open mind to look for the positives that result from having the horrendous skin condition I suffered with, not just in my teens, but for most of my adult life, at least until modern pharmacology provided a chemical weapon, a medicine that allowed me to win the battle against cystic acne.

I cannot say whether anyone's skin condition that looks like acne is an indication of any disease which needs to be cured, or is evidence of an out-of-balance condition of the body's natural processes which should be more carefully regulated, or whether it might be a positive indicator that the body is already being stimulated to keep primed a necessary and active immuno-defensive system.

The way the human body works is a mystery, about which more is learned daily, both by the scientific community and by those who simply pay attention to the functioning of their own bodies.

However, since I know that people do try to self-medicate and do look for solutions to what they perceive is a problem, even where the medical community does not hold all the answers, I provide this diet, which I found helpful in calming my terrible skin condition in my teens.

This diet was prescribed to me by a doctor fifty years ago and was successful in controlling my own cystic acne, which had been causing me great pain and much misery. When I stopped following this diet, my acne returned, but it was not as bad as it had been, as I continued to try to limit foods that I considered were probably "bad" for my skin. Throughout my life, whenever the condition of my skin was particularly troubling me, I have found relief in following this diet for a limited time, from a few days to up to two weeks, though I found it difficult to avoid all of my favorite foods for any longer than that.

You may wish to try this Anti-Acne Diet, at least once, to make an attempt to relieve symptoms of a skin condition which might be improved by a change in diet.

To begin, for two weeks only, eliminate from your diet all foods on the "List to Avoid."

If your skin condition improves, you might try bringing back into your diet some of your most favorite foods and drinks in limited quantities. You may be able to identify something that you are ingesting which is irritating to your skin.

A balanced diet seems to be crucial to maintaining good health and proper physical development. In school I was taught that the body's first line of defense against illness and bacteria is the skin, which a doctor once told me works best in unbroken condition.

Science has yet to unlock all the secrets of health and longevity. No doctor is fully informed, and often, a little knowledge is a dangerous thing.

Proceed with this diet at your own risk!

The Basic Concept: What to Avoid and What to Ingest

When selecting anything to eat or drink, avoid everything artificially flavored or colored, all processed foods, spices, anything that makes you sweat, and fats or oils except those found in good foods listed below.

Eat plenty of plain baked or boiled proteins: poached, hard-boiled, or soft-boiled eggs; plain tuna, baked salmon and other fish; baked or grilled skinless plain chicken, lean beef, or lean pork.

Eat plenty of fresh fruits: apples, oranges, grapefruit, bananas, and pears.

Eat plenty of fresh green, leafy vegetables and other fresh vegetables: lettuce, carrots, celery, cucumbers, tomatoes.

Eat plenty of baked or boiled vegetables: zucchini, yellow squash, potatoes, brown rice, corn, peas.

Drink water.

List of Foods and Drinks to Specifically Avoid

- salt, pepper, ketchup, mustard, spices, spicy food
- alcohol, cigarettes, caffeine, coffee, tea, cocoa, soda or other carbonated beverages, stimulants
- oil, salad dressing, mayonnaise
- butter, cream, whipped cream, milk fats, milk, ice cream, cheese, other milk products
- nuts, peanut butter
- sugars, corn syrup, pancake syrup, jelly, jam, molasses, sherbet
- chocolate, candy, cookies, cake, doughnuts, gum, other sweets
- artificial ingredients, flavorings, colorings
- yeast, baking powder, baking soda, other additives
- spaghetti or other pasta, white rice, bread, rolls, English muffins, bagels
- pizza, bacon, hot dogs, ground meat, chicken skin, canned vegetables or soups, sauces, frozen prepared foods, other processed foods

FOLLOW-UP NOTES

Write in this space your own experience with the Anti-Acne Diet, to record what, if anything, has worked for you.

THE RECIPES

Bran Muffins

1/3 C salted butter, plus enough to grease muffin tins
1 C whole milk
1 1/2 C All-Bran bran cereal
1 1/3 C white wheat flour
1 tsp salt
1 T baking powder
1/2 C granulated cane sugar
1 banana, ripe, but not too overripe
1 large egg
1 C chopped walnuts
1/4 C semi-sweet chocolate chips

***

Preheat oven to 400 degrees F.
Allow the butter to come to room temperature.
Butter the tins to make 24 mini-muffins.
Add milk to cereal in a large bowl. Let stand 2 minutes.
In a separate bowl, combine the dry ingredients: flour, salt,
    baking powder, and sugar.
Lightly mash most of the banana on a plate with the tines of a
    fork. Cut the rest into small, unmashed chunks.
Add egg and 1/3 C butter to cereal. Stir just to combine.
Add dry ingredients. Stir just to combine.
Add banana and stir gently to fold in.
Fold in walnuts and chocolate chips.
Fill muffin tins. Don't smooth the tops, but leave the surfaces
    uneven.
Bake at 400 degrees F about 20 minutes until well-browned.
Remove from tins. Cool completely.
Keep in air-tight container.

Corn Muffins

1/4 C (1/2 stick) unsalted butter, plus enough to grease the
    muffin tins
1 C white wheat flour
1 tsp salt
1 T baking powder
1 C corn meal
1/4 C granulated cane sugar
1 large egg
1 C whole milk

***

Preheat oven to 425 degrees F.
Butter mini-muffin tins.
In a large bowl, combine the dry ingredients: flour, salt, baking
    powder, corn meal, sugar.
Cut butter into dry ingredients.
In a separate bowl, stir together wet ingredients: egg, milk.
Add wet ingredients to dry ingredients. Stir, just to combine.
Fill tins so that each mini-muffin is 2/3 full.
Bake at 425 degrees F about 15 to 18 minutes until muffins are
    just starting to brown. Don't undercook.
Remove from tins.

Fluffy Muffins

1/4 C (1/2 stick) unsalted butter, plus enough to grease the
    muffin tins
2 C white wheat flour
1 tsp salt
1 T baking powder
1/4 C granulated cane sugar
1 large egg
1 C whole milk

***

Preheat oven to 425 degrees F.
Butter mini-muffin tins.
In a large bowl, combine the dry ingredients: flour, salt, baking
    powder, sugar.
Cut butter into dry ingredients.
In a separate bowl, stir together wet ingredients: egg, milk.
Add wet ingredients to dry ingredients. Stir, just to combine.
Fill tins so that each mini-muffin is 2/3 full.
Bake at 425 degrees F about 12 to 15 minutes until muffins are
    just starting to brown. Don't undercook.
Remove from tins.

Banana Bread

1/3 C salted butter, plus enough to grease the pan
1 3/4 C white wheat flour
3/4 tsp salt
1/2 tsp baking soda
1 1/4 tsp baking powder
2/3 C granulated cane sugar
2 large eggs
2 T whole milk
3 bananas, ripe, but not too overripe
1 C chopped walnuts
1 C mini semi-sweet chocolate chips
cinnamon sugar

***

Preheat oven to 350 degrees F.
Butter a loaf pan.
Combine dry ingredients: flour, salt, baking soda, baking powder, cane sugar.
In a separate large bowl, stir together wet ingredients: 1/3 C butter, eggs, milk.
Lightly mash most of the banana on a plate with the tines of a fork. Cut the rest into small, unmashed chunks.
Stir dry ingredients and bananas into wet ingredients just until combined.
Add walnuts and chocolate chips.
Pour into loaf pan.
Sprinkle cinnamon sugar as topping.
Bake at 350 degrees F about 60 to 70 minutes until a knife inserted into the center comes out clean.
Allow to cool a few minutes before removing from pan.
Cool completely before wrapping in aluminum foil to store.

Corn Bread

1 C white wheat flour
1 tsp salt
1 T baking powder
1 C corn meal
1/4 C granulated cane sugar
1/4 C (1/2 stick) unsalted butter, plus enough to grease the pan
1 large egg
1 C whole milk
2 T sour cream

***

Preheat oven to 425 degrees F.
Butter 9" x 9" glass cake pan.
In a large bowl, combine the dry ingredients: flour, salt, baking
    powder, corn meal, sugar.
Cut 1/4 C butter into dry ingredients.
In a separate bowl, stir together wet ingredients: egg, milk.
Add wet ingredients to dry ingredients. Stir, just to combine.
Add sour cream. Stir, just to combine.
Spread in cake pan.
Bake at 425 degrees F about 20 to 25 minutes until well-
    browned.
Serve with butter.

Gingerbread

vegetable oil, for pan
parchment paper, for pan
1/2 C plus 2 T unsalted butter
1/2 C plus 2 T brown sugar
3/4 C plus 1 T light corn syrup
3/4 C plus 1 T molasses
2 tsp fresh ginger, finely grated
1 tsp cinnamon
1 C plus 2 T whole milk
2 large eggs
1 tsp baking soda
2 T warm water
2 C white wheat flour
1 T lemon juice
1/2 C plus 2 T confectioner's sugar, sifted
up to 1 T warm water

***

Preheat oven to 325 degrees F.
Oil a 12"x8"x2" cake pan and line it with parchment paper.
Melt butter, sugar, syrup, molasses, ginger, and cinnamon.
Turn off heat.
Stir in the milk and eggs.
Combine the baking soda with the warm water and add that, too.
Add flour, beating very well, to make a liquid batter.
Bake at 325 degrees F about 45 minutes to an hour, until risen and firm. Allow to cool.
Whisk lemon juice into confectioner's sugar.
Gradually add water just until it becomes a thick icing.
Spread icing over cooled gingerbread.
Allow to set before cutting.

Lemon Bread

1/2 C (1stick) salted butter, plus enough to grease the pan
1 C granulated cane sugar
2 large eggs
1/2 C whole milk
1 1/2 C white wheat flour
1/2 tsp salt
1 tsp baking powder
zest of 1 lemon
juice of 1 lemon, for glaze
1/4 C granulated cane sugar, for glaze

***

Preheat oven to 350 degrees F.
Butter 5"x9" loaf pan, or several smaller loaf pans.
Cream butter and granulated sugar.
Mix in eggs, 1 at a time.
Mix in milk.
Stir together dry ingredients: flour salt, baking powder.
Add dry ingredients and lemon zest to wet ingredients.
Bake at 350 degrees F about 55 to 60 minutes until a toothpick
    inserted into the center comes out clean.
Make the lemon glaze while the bread is baking.
Mix lemon juice and sugar.
Warm in saucepan until dissolved.
While "Lemon Bread" is still hot, poke holes in the top, and
    then pour glaze evenly over the top of the bread.
While the bread is still hot from the oven, poke holes in the top
    and pour Lemon Glaze evenly over the top. It soaks into the
    holes poked into the top of the bread.

Zucchini Bread

vegetable oil for parchment paper to line loaf pan
3 2/3 C white wheat flour
1 1/4 tsp salt
1 tsp baking soda
1/4 baking powder
3/4 T cinnamon
2 2/3 C granulated cane sugar
15 oz zucchini, grated
1 C hazelnuts, toasted, skinned, finely chopped
4 large eggs
1/2 C vegetable oil
1 T pure vanilla extract

***

Preheat oven to 350 degrees F.
Oil parchment paper.
Line loaf pan with oiled parchment paper.
Combine dry ingredients: flour, salt, baking soda, baking powder, cinnamon, sugar; plus zucchini, hazelnuts.
Combine wet ingredients: eggs, oil, vanilla.
Add dry ingredients to wet ingredients and mix just to combine.
Pour batter into pan.
Bake at 350 degrees F about 1 hour 30 minutes until a toothpick inserted into the center comes out clean.

Chocolate Bread

vegetable oil, to grease the bowl
2 T yeast
1/4 C water, warm (105-115 degrees F)
3/4 C whole milk, scalded
1/3 C salted butter
1/4 C granulated cane sugar
1 tsp salt
2 large eggs
1/2 tsp pure vanilla extract
3 1/2 C bread flour
6 oz semi-sweet chocolate chips
1/2 C walnuts, chopped
dried fruits
1 large egg, beaten, for dough
1 large egg, beaten, for topping

***

Preheat oven to 350 degrees F.
Grease large bowl, for rising dough.
Dissolve yeast in water. Set aside.
Mix together milk, butter, sugar, and salt.
Beat in 2 eggs and vanilla.
Stir in yeast.
Gradually add flour, beating well.
Knead 8 minutes.
Place dough in greased bowl, turn once, cover.
Allow to rise 1 1/2 hours.
Knead 1 minute.
Roll into 14" x 22" rectangle.
Sprinkle with chocolate chips, walnuts, dried fruits.
Roll into 22" log. Seal seam.
Form into ring. Seal ends.
Place on baking sheet, seam side down.

Chocolate Bread (cont.)

At 1" intervals, cut 2/3 of the way through the ring, leaving the center intact.

Gently twist each section.

Cover. Let rise 1 hour, until doubled.

Brush top with beaten egg.

Bake at 350 degrees F about 25 to 30 minutes.

French Bread

parchment paper, for baking sheet
1 C water
water in spritzer bottle (like those used for spraying the leaves
    of houseplants)
3 1/2 C bread flour
2 1/4 tsp salt
2 1/4 tsp (1 packet) dry yeast
1 1/2 C warm water (120 to 130 degrees F)

***

Preheat oven to 450 degrees F.
Place baking stone on top oven rack.
Place broiling pan on rack 4" beneath baking stone.
Add 1 C water to broiling pan.
Line baking sheet with parchment paper.
Stir together all of the ingredients, except 1 C flour.
Knead the dough about 5 minutes while adding, a little at a
    time, as much of the remaining flour as needed to make a
    smooth-surfaced dough that is soft and a little bit sticky.
Let the dough rise 3 hours. Punch down the dough.
Let the dough rise 1 1/2 hours.
Separate dough into two balls, folding each one over itself.
Let the dough rise, covered with cloth, about 5 minutes.
Shape each ball into a loaf, place on baking sheet lined with
    parchment paper.
Cover with cloth and let rise 1 1/2 hour.
Transfer dough to a baker's peel.
Slash the loaves diagonally, about 1 inch apart.
Spray the loaves with water using the spritzer.
Slide the loaves into the oven on the preheated stone.
Add 1 C water to the broiling pan.
Bake at 450 degrees F about 25 minutes until golden brown.
Spray the loaves with water at 3-minute intervals while baking.
Allow bread to cool 2 hours before cutting.

Fry Bread for Salt Fish

3 C water, warm (about 105 degrees F)
1/2 tsp yeast
1 T salt
6 1/2 C bread flour, plus more, for hands and for dusting table
vegetable oil, for bowl and for skillet

***

Mix water, yeast, and salt.
Add flour, all at once.
Stir, until all of the flour is mixed in.
With floured hands, form a ball.
Place ball in very large oiled bowl.
Cover bowl with cloth.
Set bowl in warm place (at least room temperature).
Allow to rise 12 hours.
Refrigerate until needed.
Dust table with flour.
With floured hands, and using one bit of the dough at a time,
    form a ball from dough.
Roll the ball flat, about 1/4" thick, making a 6" circle.
Cover bottom of cast iron skillet with thin layer of oil.
Heat skillet to sizzling hot.
Fry bread on hot skillet 2 to 3 minutes, until golden brown on
    the underside.
Flip bread with spatula.
Fry the second side for a shorter amount of time, about 1 minute
    or more, until golden brown on the underside.
Pop the larger bubbles.
Remove from skillet to brown paper, to absorb oil.

German Bread

vegetable oil, for bowl
2 T yeast
1/4 C water, warm (105-115 degrees F)
3/4 C whole milk, scalded
1/3 C salted butter
1/4 C granulated cane sugar
1 tsp salt
2 large eggs
1/2 tsp pure vanilla extract
3 1/2 C bread flour
6 oz dried fruits
1/2 C walnuts, chopped
1 large egg, beaten, for fruit, nut inner layer
1 large egg, beaten, for topping

***

Grease large bowl, for rising dough.
Dissolve yeast in water. Set aside.
Mix together milk, butter, sugar, and salt.
Beat in eggs and vanilla. Stir in yeast.
Gradually add flour, beating well. Knead 8 minutes.
Place dough in greased bowl, turn once, cover.
Allow to rise 1 1/2 hours. Knead 1 minute.
Preheat oven to 350 degrees F.
Roll into 14" x 22" rectangle.
Sprinkle with chocolate chips and walnuts.
Roll into 22" log. Seal seam. Form into ring. Seal ends.
Place on baking sheet, seam side down.
At 1" intervals, cut 2/3 of the way through the ring, leaving the
    center intact.
Gently twist each section.
Cover. Let rise 1 hour, until doubled.
Brush top with egg.
Bake at 350 degrees F about 25 to 30 minutes.

Pumpernickel Bread

<< ingredients >>

2 1/2 tsp yeast
1 1/2 C bread flour
1 C rye flour
1 C whole wheat flour
1 1/2 T vital wheat gluten
1 1/8 C water
1 1/2 T salted butter
1/3 C molasses
3 T cocoa powder
1 1/2 tsp salt
1 T caraway seeds

***

Place yeast in corner of bread pan of automatic bread machine.
Layer other ingredients on top of yeast.
Press the start button.
For a lovely presentation, scoop out bread to make a bread bowl
to hold "Spinach-Artichoke Dip." Serve with cubes of bread
to eat with dip. A great party food!

Sesame Seed Bread

2 C bread flour, for poolish
1/4 tsp yeast, for poolish
1 C cool water (65 degrees F), for poolish
1/2 C cool water (65 degrees F), for dough
1 1/2 C bread flour, for dough
2 tsp yeast, for dough
1 1/2 tsp salt, for dough
1 C bread flour, to add to dough, adding just enough to make
    smooth dough
wooden cutting board
parchment paper, for wooden cutting board
cornmeal, for parchment paper
water, to moisten the loaf with the hands
1 large egg
1/4 C sesame seeds
aluminum foil, to tent rising loaf
baking stone
baking sheet with sides (will hold 2 C water)
cornmeal, for baking stone
2 C water, for baking sheet while baking

***

Trust me, this one is worth it.
Study this recipe before you start. Practice making it until you
    get good at it. Then you'll know you can cook anything by
    following a recipe carefully!
For this recipe, prepare the bread starter, called a "poolish," at
    least 12 hours before making the bread.
Stir together poolish ingredients: flour, yeast, water.
Mix to form a dough.
Cover loosely, let rest at room temperature for 12-16 hours.
Gently mix the poolish and the water for dough, until softened.
Combine the other ingredients for dough: flour, yeast, salt.
Add to poolish.

Sesame Seed Bread (cont.)

Knead the dough about 5 minutes while adding, a little at a time, as much of the remaining 1 C flour as needed to make a smooth-surfaced dough.

Place in bowl, cover bowl with dishtowel, let rise 30 minutes.

Fold all four sides of dough into the middle and turn the dough over.

Place in bowl, cover again, let rise 30 minutes for the second time.

Fold all four sides of dough into the middle and turn the dough over for the second time.

Place in bowl, cover again, let rise 30 minutes for the third time.

Line wooden cutting board with parchment paper.

Sprinkle cornmeal on the parchment paper.

Spread dough out into a long rectangle.

Using a knife, from the bottom of the rectangle to the top, cut the dough to divide it into thirds; but don't cut the slices all the way through to the top, keep the tops of the three all connected.

Pull each of the three parts to stretch it out and down and a little apart from the others, and pull and roll the dough between the hands, forming the dough into three 20-inch ropes, still attached at the top.

Wet your hands with water. Using the hands and wetting with additional water as needed, moisten the entire dough surface with water.

Braid the three ropes together, pinching the three loose ends together at the bottom and tucking the pinched parts underneath to hide them.

Pulling the top and bottom ends, lengthen the loaf.

Shape the ends nicely, to make it look like a braided loaf.

Place loaf on wooden cutting board lined with parchment paper and sprinkled with cornmeal.

Sesame Seed Bread (cont.)

With wet hands, moisten the top and sides of the entire loaf
again.

Beat egg, then brush top and sides of entire loaf with beaten
egg.

Sprinkle top and sides of loaf with sesame seeds.

Cover loaf with an aluminum foil tent (constructed large enough
to allow the bread room to rise without touching the foil)
and let rise 1 1/2 hours.

Place baking stone on top oven rack.

Place on the rack below, at least 4 inches below the baking
stone, a baking sheet with sides. (The sides must be high
enough for the baking sheet to be able to hold the 2 C water
which will be added in a later step.)

Preheat oven to 450 degrees F.

Open the oven and slide out the top shelf. Sprinkle cornmeal on
the baking stone.

Lift the loaf from the parchment paper carefully and place it
onto the cornmeal on the preheated baking stone. Slide the
top shelf back into the oven.

Add 2 C water to the baking sheet. Close the oven door.

Lower the oven temperature to 425 degrees F.

Bake 35 minutes at 425 degrees F until bread is golden brown.

Allow bread to cool in oven with door open ajar 30 minutes.

Remove from oven and cool on rack before cutting.

Sourdough Bread

1 C sourdough starter
1/2 C bread flour, to feed sourdough
1/3 C water, to feed sourdough
parchment paper, for baking sheet
5 C bread flour
2 1/2 tsp salt
2 tsp yeast
1 T granulated cane sugar
1 1/2 C warm water (120 to 130 degrees F)

***

Keep sourdough starter on hand.
Feed the sourdough first with 1/2 C flour and 1/3 C water.
Whisk together, cover lightly, let sit 12 hours.
Reserve half the sourdough starter, then make this recipe usung the other half.
Combine starter with bread ingredients: flour, salt, yeast, sugar, water.
Knead to form a smooth dough.
Let the dough rise 1 1/2 hours.
Divide dough and shape into two loaves.
Line baking sheet with parchment paper.
Place loaves on parchment paper on baking sheet.
Let the loaves rise 1 hour.
Preheat oven to 425 degrees F.
Spray the loaves with lukewarm water using a spritzer.
Slash the loaves diagonally, twice.
Spray the loaves with water using the spritzer.
Bake 25-30 minutes at 425 degrees F until a very deep golden brown.
Allow bread to cool on a rack.

White Bread

2 T yeast
3 C bread flour
1 tsp salt
1 T salted butter
1 T olive oil
2 T molasses
1 tsp granulated cane sugar
1 large egg
1 C whole milk

***

Place yeast in corner of bread pan of automatic bread machine.
Layer other ingredients on top of yeast, in order.
Select:"large loaf," "dark crust," "bake 4 hours."
Press the start button.

Whole Wheat Bread

1 1/2 tsp yeast
3 C bread flour
1 1/4 C whole wheat flour
2 tsp salt
1/3 C salted butter
1 C whole milk

***

Place yeast in corner of bread pan of automatic bread machine.
Layer other ingredients on top of yeast, in order.
Press the start button.
To store, first allow loaf to cool completely before covering,
    then add a cotton cloth to the container to absorb moisture.

Brownies

(optional) 1 C dried cherries
(optional) brandy, for soaking cherries
1 1/2 C white wheat flour
1/2 tsp baking powder
1/4 tsp salt
1/2 C (1 stick) salted butter
1/2 C Crisco shortening
3 1-oz squares unsweetened chocolate
4 large eggs
2 C granulated cane sugar
1 tsp pure vanilla extract
1 C walnuts, chopped
(optional) 1/2 C warmed peanut butter
powdered sugar, for dusting the top

***

(optional): Soak cherries in brandy for an hour. Drain.
Combine dry ingredients: flour, baking powder, salt.
In saucepan, melt together: butter, shortening, chocolate: Cool
    slightly.
Beat the eggs together, then whisk some of the egg into the
    chocolate a little at a time: using about a quarter of the
    beaten egg each time, do this 4 times to incorporate all the
    egg.
Stir in: sugar, vanilla, walnuts, (optional) cherries.
Spread into in an ungreased 9" x 13" glass pan.
(optional): Warm peanut butter and swirl it into the brownies.
Bake for 15 to 20 minutes at 350 degrees F.
When cooled, dust with powdered sugar.
Let cool 2 minutes on baking sheet.
Remove to brown paper to cool completely.

Chocolate Chip Cookies

2 1/4 C white wheat flour
1 tsp baking soda
1 tsp salt
1 C (2 sticks) salted butter
3/4 C granulated cane sugar
3/4 C brown sugar
2 large eggs
1 tsp pure vanilla extract
2 C semi-sweet chocolate chips
1 C walnuts, chopped

***

Preheat oven to 375 degrees F.
Combine dry ingredients: flour, baking soda, salt.
In mixing bowl, cream butter, sugar, and brown sugar.
Add eggs, one at a time, beating well after each addition.
Gradually beat in dry ingredients.
Stir in chocolate chips and walnuts.
Drop by rounded tablespoonfuls onto baking sheets.
Bake at 375 degrees F about 9 to 11 minutes until golden
    brown.
Let cool 2 minutes on baking sheet.
Remove to brown paper to cool completely.

Christmas Cookies (Sugar Cookies)

2 1/2 C white wheat flour, plus flour for dusting
1 tsp baking soda
1 tsp cream of tartar
1 C (2 sticks) salted butter
1 1/2 C confectioner's sugar
1 large egg
1 tsp pure vanilla extract
1/2 tsp almond extract
sugar sprinkles, for decorating
cinnamon bits, for decorating
Lifesaver candies, crushed, for decorating

***

Preheat oven to 375 degrees F.
Combine dry ingredients: flour, baking soda, cream of tartar.
Cream butter and confectioner's sugar.
Add egg, vanilla, and almond extract. Mix well.
Pat into balls, flatten, seal in ZIPLOC baggies.
Cool dough in refrigerator at least 3 hours.
Flour the surface of the table, the rolling pin, and hands.
Place dough on table, dust with flour.
Roll out dough flat and to an even thickness, less than 1/4 inch thick. Roll out to as thin as possible, just thick enough so cookies do not fall apart. Make all cookies the same thickness, or some will burn and some will undercook.
Dip cookie cutters in flour, cut cookies, and remove to baking sheet.
Collect leftover dough scraps, press into a ball, and keep making cookies until all the dough is used up.
If dough gets too warm and sticky, return it to Ziploc bags and chill before making more cookies.
Decorate cookies with sugar sprinkles, cinnamon bits, and Lifesaver candies.
Bake at 375 degrees F about 6 to 8 minutes until the underside of the cookie is light brown. Don't undercook.

Cranberry Cookies

vegetable oil, for cookie sheet
2 1/2 C cranberries, fresh, coarsely chopped
3 C white wheat flour
1/2 tsp salt
1/4 tsp baking soda
1 tsp baking powder
1/2 C (1 stick) salted butter
1 C granulated cane sugar
3/4 C brown sugar
1 large egg
1/4 C whole milk
2 T orange juice
1 C walnuts, chopped

***

Preheat oven to 375 degrees F.

Grease cookie sheet with oil.

Cutting cranberries into quarters by hand rather than using a machine helps the cranberries keep their shape and texture.

Combine dry ingredients: flour, salt, baking soda, baking powder.

Cream butter, sugar, and brown sugar.

Stir in egg, milk, and orange juice.

Stir in dry ingredients.

Stir in cranberries and walnuts.

Drop by rounded teaspoonfuls about 2 inches apart onto cookie sheet.

Bake at 375 degrees F about 10 to 15 minutes until the cookies are slightly crisped on the bottom and not too soft.

These cookies do not last long once they come out of the oven, so wait by the kitchen door so you don't miss out.

Gingerbread Cookies and Gingerbread House

vegetable oil, for pan
parchment paper, for pan
1/2 C (1 stick) salted butter
1/2 C brown sugar
1/4 C molasses
2 tsp ginger
1 tsp cinnamon
2 large eggs
2 C water
2 tsp baking soda
4 C white wheat flour
1 recipe "Gingerbread House Cement"
Decorations: icing, sprinkles, mini-marshmallows, M&Ms, gum
    drops, jelly beans, Skittles, Life Savers, chocolate-covered
    graham crackers, licorice, chocolate chips, nonpareils,
    candy canes
Design "Gingerbread House. Cut paper templates for walls and
    roof. Assembled roof must overlap the sides of the house.

***

Preheat oven to 325 degrees F.
Oil a baking sheet and line with parchment paper.
Melt butter, sugar, molasses, ginger, and cinnamon.
Turn off heat.
Stir in eggs, water, baking soda. Add flour, beating very well.
Roll dough to 1/4 inch.
Cut pieces to make pieces for "Gingerbread House" or cookies.
Place on prepared parchment paper.
Bake at 325 degrees F until firm. Do not overcook.
Use "Gingerbread House Cement" to stick together the walls
    and roof of the "Gingerbread House."
Allow cement to set a bit before sticking on candies with more
    cement.

Lemon Bars

1 C white wheat flour
1/4 C confectioner's sugar
1/2 C (1 stick) unsalted butter
2 large eggs
3/4 C granulated cane sugar
1/2 tsp lemon peel
3 T lemon juice
2 T white wheat flour
1/4 tsp baking powder
confectioner's sugar, for topping

***

Preheat oven to 350 degrees F.
Combine dry ingredients: flour, confectioner's sugar.
Cut in butter into dry ingredients.
Add to 8" x 8" baking pan.
Bake the empty crust about 10 to 12 minutes at 350 degrees F.
Beat eggs well.
Add sugar, lemon peel, and lemon juice.
Beat about 8 to 10 minutes, until thick and smooth.
Stir in dry ingredients: flour, baking powder; just until
    moistened.
Pour over crust.
Bake the filled crust at 350 degrees F about 20 to 25 minutes.
Cool.
Sift confectioner's sugar on top.

Oatmeal Cookies

1 1/2 C white wheat flour
1 tsp baking soda
1/2 tsp salt
1 tsp cinnamon
1 C (2 sticks) salted butter
1 C brown sugar
1/2 C granulated cane sugar
2 large eggs
1 tsp pure vanilla extract
3 C oatmeal, Quaker original, plain, dry oats
1 C raisins, dried cranberries, and/or walnuts

***

Preheat oven to 350 degrees F.
Combine dry ingredients: flour, baking soda, salt, cinnamon.
Cream butter and sugars.
Add eggs and vanilla. Beat well.
Mix in dry ingredients.
Stir in oatmeal, raisins, cranberries, walnuts.
Drop by rounded teaspoonfuls onto cookie sheets.
Bake at 350 degrees F about 8 to 10 minutes for chewy cookies,
    or about 11 to 12 minutes for crispy cookies.

Oh My! Cookies

vegetable oil, for cookie sheet
parchment paper, for cookie sheet
1/2 C granulated cane sugar
2 tsp cinnamon
2 1/4 C white wheat flour
1 tsp baking soda
1/2 tsp salt
2 tsp cream of tartar
1 C (2 sticks) salted butter
1 1/2 C granulated cane sugar
2 large eggs

***

Preheat oven to 350 degrees F.
Grease cookie sheet with oil, or line with parchment paper.
Mix ingredients for cinnamon sugar coating: sugar, cinnamon.
Cream butter.
Add sugar and cream until fluffy.
Mix in eggs, one at a time.
Add dry ingredients, one-half at a time, mixing in thoroughly.
Chill 30 to 60 minutes.
Measure 1 T dough, roll into a ball, cover in coating, and place
    on baking sheet.
Bake at 350 degrees F about 13 to 16 minutes until outside of
    cookie feels slightly firm to the touch.

Toasted Almond Biscotti

1 C almonds, whole, blanched
2 3/4 C white wheat flour
1/2 tsp baking soda
3/4 tsp baking powder
pinch salt
4 large eggs
1 C granulated cane sugar
1 tsp almond extract

***

Toast almonds on baking sheet at 350 degrees F for 15 minutes,
    stirring twice.
Lightly beat eggs, reserving 2 T in a bowl in the refrigerator.
    For the first baking, it will be used to brush the top of the
    loaf to create a glaze.
Beat sugar and almond extract into remaining eggs.
Add dry ingredients: flour, baking soda, baking powder, and
    salt.
Stir to form a very soft dough.
Divide the dough in half and place one piece on a well-floured
    work surface.
With floured hands, pat into a 6-inch square.
Scatter half of the almonds on the dough and press them into the
    surface.
Roll the dough into a 2-inch cylinder, 12 to 15 inches long.
Place on baking sheet.
Repeat with remaining dough.
Brush the tops with reserved egg.
For this, the first of two bakings, bake at 350 degrees F about
    15 minutes until golden and firm to the touch.
Transfer these half-baked cookies to a cutting board and cut on
    an angle into slices one-half-inch thick.
Stand up slices on baking sheet lined with parchment paper.

>>

Toasted Almond Biscotti (cont.)

For the second and final baking, bake at 350 degrees F about 20 minutes until biscotti are crisp and dry.

These twice-baked cookies sound complicated, but once you get a handle on what the consistency of the cookie log is supposed to be after each round of baking, they turn out perfect every time.

The raw dough is very soft and sticky. The first time it is baked, the dough solidifies just enough to make the log hang together so that it may be sliced nicely, at an angle.

The second baking is to crisp up the cookie into the lovely biscotti crunchiness you dream of. Stand the cookies up on their edge, and line them all up in a row, standing apart and not touching, like in social distancing.

This special treat is perfect for gift-giving. Fill a large, lidded ceramic jar with biscotti, add a red bow, and listen to the squeals of delight when the recipient of your grab bag present realizes they've hit the jackpot!

Angel Food Cake

1 1/2 C superfine sugar, divided
1 C sifted cake flour
12 large egg whites, room temperature
1/4 tsp salt
1 1/2 tsp cream of tartar
1 tsp pure vanilla extract
1/2 tsp almond extract

***

Preheat oven to 350 degrees F.
Sift together 1/2 C sugar and flour.
Beat egg whites, salt, cream of tartar, vanilla, and almond
    extract until very foamy.
Slowly add 1 C sugar.
Beat until stiff, glossy peaks form.
Sift half the flour mixture over the eggs, fold in gently with
    rubber spatula.
Repeat.
Transfer batter to ungreased 10-inch tube pan.
Bake at 350 degrees F about 35 to 40 minutes until a toothpick
    inserted into the center comes out clean.
Cool upside down on wine bottle.

Carrot Cake

unsalted butter, for pan
white wheat flour, for pan
2 C white wheat flour
1 tsp baking soda
1/2 tsp salt
2 tsp cinnamon
2 C granulated cane sugar
1 1/2 C olive oil
4 large eggs
3 C carrots, grated
1 C coconut, shredded
1 C pineapple, crushed, drained
1 C walnuts, chopped
1 recipe "Cream Cheese Icing"

***

Preheat oven to 350 degrees F.
Butter and flour Bundt pan.
Combine dry ingredients: flour baking soda, salt, cinnamon.
Beat sugar with olive oil until thick and well blended.
Beat in eggs.
Beat in dry ingredients.
Mix in carrots, coconut, pineapple, and walnuts.
Bake at 350 degrees F about 55 minutes until a toothpick
    inserted into the center comes out clean.
Cool 15 minutes in pan on wire rack.
Loosen edges with butter knife.
Remove from pan.
Cool completely before icing with "Cream Cheese Icing."

Cheesecake

9" springform pan
18 whole graham crackers
1/4 C light brown sugar
1/2 tsp kosher salt
1/2 tsp cinnamon
3/4 C unsalted butter, melted
4 8-oz pkgs Philadelphia cream cheese, original
1/2 C sour cream
1 C granulated cane sugar
1 tsp pure vanilla extract
1/2 tsp kosher salt
4 large eggs, plus 1 large egg yolk
1/4 C white wheat flour

***

Preheat oven to 325 degrees F.
Crush graham crackers to make fine crumbs. Suggestion: put in
    sealed Ziploc bag and smash with rolling pin.
Combine in bowl: crumbs, brown sugar, salt, cinnamon.
Add melted butter. Mix well with fingers until small clumps
    hold together.
Press crust into 9" springform pan. Cover the bottom of the pan
    and at least 1 1/2" up the sides. Flatten the bottom of the
    crust as even as possible by pressing it with a glass
    measuring cup.
Bake at 325 degrees F about 20 to 25 minutes until crust is set
    and the edges are just starting to brown. Take pan out of
    oven.
Reset oven to 300 degrees F.
Combine in bowl of electric mixer: cream cheese, sour cream,
    sugar, vanilla, salt.
Beat on high speed about 4 minutes until completely smooth.
Reduce mixer speed to medium.

Cheesecake (cont.)

Add eggs and yolk, one at a time mixing completely each time.
Reduce mixer speed to low.
Add flour. Beat just to blend until there are no lumps.
Pour into pan. It is okay if the filling goes above the top edge of
the crust.
Bake at 300 degrees F about 60 to 70 minutes until the edges of
the cheesecake are completely set and the middle of the
cheesecake wobbles just slightly.
Turn off the oven, but do not remove cheesecake from the oven
for ten minutes.
Remove cheesecake to a wire rack to cool to room temperature.
Refrigerate until totally set, at least 6 hours, or overnight.

Cranberry Sour Cream Coffee Cake

vegetable oil, for tube pan
salted butter, for tube pan
1/4 C almonds, chopped
1/2 C salted butter
2 C white wheat flour, for batter
1/2 tsp baking soda, for batter
1 1/4 tsp baking powder, for batter
1/4 tsp salt, for batter
1 C granulated cane sugar, for batter
1 tsp pure vanilla extract, for batter
2 large eggs, for batter
1 C sour cream, for batter
1 C Ocean Spray whole berry cranberry sauce
1/2 C white wheat flour, for topping
1/3 C granulated cane sugar, for topping
1/4 C almonds, chopped, for topping
1/3 C salted butter, melted, for topping
1/4 tsp pure vanilla extract, for topping

***

Preheat oven to 350 degrees F.
Oil completely a 10-inch tube pan.
Spread butter on the bottom of the pan. Add almonds.
Combine dry ingredients: flour, baking soda, baking powder,
    salt.
Cream: butter, sugar. Beat 2 minutes until well mixed.
Beat in vanilla.
Beat in eggs, beating 1 to 2 minutes, until well mixed.
Alternately beat in dry ingredients and sour cream, beating 1 to
    2 more minutes, until batter is well mixed.
Make 3 layers in the tube pan: half the batter, the cranberry
    sauce, the rest of the batter.
Mix topping ingredients: flour, sugar, almonds, butter, vanilla.

Cranberry Sour Cream Coffee Cake (cont.)

Distribute topping over cake.

Bake at 350 degrees F about 70 to 85 minutes until a toothpick
inserted into the center comes out clean.

Cool 10 minutes on wire rack. Continue to cool in the tube pan.

One of my favorite recipes ever, this dessert makes the perfect
hostess gift. Delicous with coffee.

Marie's Cake (Chocolate Cake)

salted butter, for pans
white wheat flour, for pans
1 3/4 C white wheat flour
1 1/2 tsp baking soda
1 1/2 tsp baking powder
1 tsp salt
3/4 C cocoa powder
2 C granulated cane sugar
1/2 C vegetable oil
2 large eggs
1 C whole milk
2 tsp pure vanilla extract
1 C water, boiling hot
1 recipe: "Chocolate Filling"
1 recipe: chocolate "Whipped Cream"
1 C multi-colored candies

***

Preheat oven to 350 degrees F.
Butter and flour three 8-in cake pans.
Adjusting the baking time, the recipe can also be used to make
    cupcakes, a two-layer cake, or one single larger sheet cake.
Combine dry ingredients: flour, baking soda, baking powder,
    salt, cocoa powder.
Combine wet ingredients: sugar, oil, eggs, milk, vanilla.
Mix dry ingredients into wet ingredients.
Beat with mixer 2 minutes.
Stir in boiling water.
Pour into cake pans.
Bake at 350 degrees F about 28 to 35 minutes until a toothpick
    inserted into the center comes out clean.
Cool completely.
Place one cake on cake plate.

Marie's Cake (cont.)

Spread half of "Chocolate Filling" on cake.
Top with second cake.
Spread rest of filling on top of second cake.
Top with third cake.
Gently ice cake with chocolate "Whipped Cream."
Decorate top and sides with candies.
Serve immediately, or cover and chill until serving.

A delicious chocolate cake!

This is the perfect birthday cake for the chocolate lover.
Adjusting the baking time, the recipe can also be used to make
cupcakes, a two-layer cake, or one single larger sheet cake.

Mocha Cake

salted butter, for pan
white wheat flour, for pan
1 3/4 C white wheat flour
2 tsp baking soda
1 tsp baking powder
1 tsp salt
3/4 C cocoa powder
2 C granulated cane sugar
1/2 C vegetable oil
2 large eggs
1 C buttermilk
1 tsp pure vanilla extract
1 C fresh hot coffee
1 recipe "Mocha Icing"

***

Preheat oven to 350 degrees F.
Butter and flour two 9-inch cake pans.
Combine dry ingredients: flour, baking soda, baking powder,
    salt, cocoa powder.
Combine wet ingredients: sugar, oil, eggs, buttermilk, vanilla.
Mix dry ingredients into wet ingredients.
Beat with mixer 2 minutes.
Stir in fresh hot coffee.
Pour into cake pans.
Bake at 350 degrees F about 30 to 35 minutes until a toothpick
    inserted into the center comes out clean.
Cool completely.
Ice cake with "Mocha Icing."

Pineapple Upside Down Cake

10" cast iron skillet
1/3 C salted butter, for skillet
2/3 C brown sugar, for skillet
1 can (20 oz) pineapple slices in syrup, for skillet
2 T syrup, reserved from can of pineapple slices, for batter
10 maraschino cherries, for skillet
1 1/2 C white wheat flour
1 3/4 tsp baking powder
1/4 tsp salt
1/3 C salted butter
1/2 C granulated cane sugar
2 large egg yolks
1 tsp lemon peel
1 tsp lemon juice
1 tsp pure vanilla extract
1/2 C sour cream
2 large egg whites, for meringue
1/4 C granulated cane sugar, for meringue

***

Preheat oven to 350 degrees F.
Melt butter in well-seasoned 10" cast iron skillet.
Remove from heat.
Add brown sugar. Stir until well blended.
Arrange pineapple slices on butter mixture. Reserve 2T syrup.
Place maraschino cherry in the center of each pineapple slice.
In a separate bowl, combine dry ingredients: flour, baking
    powder, salt.
In a separate bowl, cream butter and sugar until fluffy.
Beat in egg yolks, lemon peel, lemon juice, and vanilla.
Add in dry ingredients, alternately with sour cream and
    pineapple syrup. Blend batter well.
Beat egg whites to soft peaks.
Gradually beat in sugar to make stiff peaks.

>>

Pineapple Upside Down Cake (cont.)

Fold meringue into batter.

Pour over pineapple slices in skillet.

Bake at 350 degrees F about 35 minutes until a toothpick inserted into the center comes out clean.

Let stand 10 minutes.

Invert onto serving plate.

Serve warm or cold.

A clever presentation dessert!

Fair warning: This cake is not for beginning cooks.

Shortcakes

parchment paper, for baking sheet
4 C white wheat flour
4 1/2 tsp baking powder
1 1/2 tsp salt
12 T salted butter, cold, cut into small pieces
2 C plus 2 T heavy cream
white wheat flour, for table and hands
parchment paper, to cover cakes
2 T heavy cream
1 large egg yolk
(optional) sugar for topping

***

Line a baking sheet with parchment paper.
Combine dry ingredients: flour, baking powder, salt.
Cut butter into dry ingredients with two knives.
Stir in cream to make dough.
Sprinkle flour on table.
Place dough on floured surface.
With floured hands, pat dough flat, to 1-inch thick.
Using a large glass, cut 10-20 cake circles.
Put the cakes on the paper, cover with more parchment paper.
Set baking sheet in refrigerator at least 20 minutes, or overnight.
When cool, remove cakes from refrigerator.
Whisk cream with egg yolk.
Brush cake tops with egg/cream mixture.
(option) Sprinkle cake tops with sugar.
Bake at 400 degrees F until golden brown in color.
Baking time depends on size of glass used as cookie cutter:
    bake small shortcakes 12 to 15 minutes, bake large
    shortcakes about 15 to 18 minutes.
Before serving, cool slightly on wire racks, about 15 minutes.

Strawberry Shortcakes

4 pints fresh-picked strawberries
1/2 C granulated cane sugar
1/4 C lemon juice, freshly squeezed
1 recipe "Shortcakes"
1 recipe: "Whipped Cream"
(optional) vanilla ice cream

***

Cut the leaves and tough tops from strawberries and discard.
Cut strawberries in half lengthwise, then slice into smaller
   pieces, cutting out and discarding any excessively hard
   white parts from the centers.
Stir together strawberries, sugar, and lemon juice.
Cover. Let stand in refrigerator 1 hour.
To serve, assemble each of the "Strawberry Shortcakes" on an
   individual cake plate.
Using a serrated knife, slice open one of the "Shortcakes."
Place bottom half of shortcake on plate, cut side up.
On top of the shortcake, add the layers: strawberries; "Whipped
   Cream"; the top half of the shortcake, cut side down; more
   strawberries; and more "Whipped Cream".
Decorate the top of each shortcake with more strawberries or
   with a single, large, uncut strawberry.
(optional) Add a scoop of vanilla ice cream on one side of the
   plate. Top with more of the cut strawberries.

Celebrate the onset of summer!

Pick your own fresh strawberries and make these simple but
scrumptious individual strawberry shortcakes.

Trifle

6 one-inch slices sponge cake
1/3 C apricot jam
1/2 C orange juice
2 C recipe "Custard"
2 C red gelatin, prepared according to package directions,
    shredded with tines of a fork
2 C recipe "Whipped Cream"

***

Spread cake slices with apricot jam.
Cut cake slices each into 4 pieces.
Arrange cake to line bottom of trifle bowl.
Using spoon, sprinkle cake with orange juice.
Top cake evenly with "Custard."
Place in refrigerator for 30 minutes, covered.
Top evenly with shredded gelatin.
Spoon "Whipped Cream" on top in a pile in the middle.

This is a beautiful and traditional presentation dessert!

Apple Pie

Good apple pie uses a combination of apples: some sweet, some tart; some soft, some crisp. For texture balance and best flavor, more than half of the apples should be crisp and tart.

fresh apples, peeled and thinly sliced into wedges less than
    about a half-inch thick
2 T lemon juice
2 T granulated cane sugar
1/4 C white wheat flour
1 recipe "Pie Crust" with whole pie top crust or lattice crust
egg wash or milk
cinnamon sugar

***

Preheat oven to 350 degrees F.
Gently mix apples, juice, and sugar.
Sprinkle flour over apples. Gently mix very well.
Fill pie crust to overflowing with as many apples as will fit.
Top with whole crust, from "Pie Crust" recipe.
Brush crust with milk or egg wash.
Sprinkle crust with cinnamon sugar.
Bake approximately 13-15 minutes at 450 degrees F until crust
    begins to brown.
Reduce heat to 350 degrees F.
Cover crusts with aluminum foil.
Bake at 350 degrees F about 1 hour 10 minutes until juice is
    bubbling and apples are soft and tender.

When apples are in season, make this every single day – life is
    short!

Spread the love, gift "Apple Pie" to friends and family.

Chocolate Pecan Pie

1/4 C (1/2 stick) salted butter, melted
1 C granulated cane sugar
3/4 C light corn syrup
3 large eggs, beaten
1 tsp pure vanilla extract
1/2 C chocolate chips
1/2 C pecans, chopped, for batter
1 recipe "Pie Crust," unbaked
1 C pecans, halves, for top of pie
1 recipe "Whipped Cream," for garnish

***

Preheat oven to 350 degrees F.
Mix together: butter, sugar, syrup, eggs, vanilla.
Add chocolate chips and chopped pecans to the batter.
Stir well.
Pour into unbaked pie crust.
Top with pecan halves.
Bake at 350 degrees F about 45 to 50 minutes, or until set.
Cool completely.
Garnish with "Whipped Cream."

With both pecans and chocolate, this pie ranks as health food in my book. Even if I have to rewrite the book.

Graham Cracker Crust

1 1/2 C graham cracker crumbs
6 T salted butter, melted, cooled
3 T granulated cane sugar

***

Preheat oven to 375 degrees F.
Combine: graham cracker crumbs, butter, sugar.
Press into the bottom and sides of a 9-inch pie plate.
Bake at 375 degrees F about 12 minutes until crust is lightly
    browned.
Cool on wire rack until completely cooled.
Make "Lemon Meringue Pie" or "Key Lime Pie."

Key Lime Pie

1 can (14 ounces) sweetened condensed milk
4 large egg yolks
1/2 C Key Lime juice
1 T grated Key Lime zest
1 recipe "Graham Cracker Crust"
1 recipe "Whipped Cream," for garnish
1 tsp grated Key Lime zest, for garnish

***

Preheat oven to 325 degrees F.
Mix milk, yolks, juice, and zest.
Pour into "Graham Cracker Crust."
Bake at 325 degrees F about 15 to 17 minutes until the center is
    set but still jiggles a bit.
Cool on wire rack.
Garnish with "Whipped Cream."
Top with lime zest.

Lemon Meringue Pie

1/4 C cornstarch
1/4 C water
2 large eggs
5 large egg yolks
1 1/2 C plus 2 T granulated cane sugar
1 pinch salt
1 C fresh lemon juice
1 1/2 T grated lemon rind
4 T unsalted butter, room temp
1 recipe "Graham Cracker Crust"
1 tsp grated lemon rind, for garnish
4 large egg whites, room temp
1/4 tsp cream of tartar
1 pinch salt
1/2 C sugar
1 tsp pure vanilla extract

***

Preheat oven to 400 degrees F.
In a small lidded jar, shake cornstarch with water to make a
    slurry.
In sauce pot, whisk eggs and sugar about 2 minutes until pale
    yellow. Whisk in: salt, juice, lemon rind, butter.
Whisk until fully incorporated. Continue to whisk.
Cook on medium heat about 7 minutes until thickened and
    deepened in color.
Remove from heat and continue to whisk 1 minute.
Fill crust. Cover with Saran Wrap. Refrigerate 1 hour.
Beat whites until foamy. Continue beating after every addition.
Add cream of tartar and salt. Mix until soft peaks form.
Add sugar slowly, 1 T at a time. Add vanilla.
Beat until light and fluffy and stiff peaks form, checking at
    thirty-second intervals.
Cover pie with meringue, forming decorative peaks.
Broil in 400 degree oven about 3 to 4 minutes until browned.

Peach Cobbler

1 can (29 oz) peaches, sliced, drained
1/4 C granulated cane sugar
1/4 C brown sugar
1 C Bisquick baking mix
1 tsp cinnamon
1/2 tsp nutmeg
1/2 C (1/2 stick) salted butter
1 C whole milk

***

Preheat oven to 375 degrees F.
Mix: peaches, sugars.
Combine dry ingredients: Bisquick, cinnamon, nutmeg.
Cut butter into dry ingredients.
Stir in milk.
Spread in 8" square glass baking dish.
Top with peaches.
Bake at 375 degrees F about 50 to 60 minutes until golden in
    color.

Peach Pie

fresh peaches, peeled and sliced
2 T lemon juice
2 T granulated cane sugar
1 recipe "Pie Crust"
egg wash or whole milk

***

Preheat oven to 375 degrees F.
Gently mix: peaches, juice, sugar.
Fill "Pie Crust" with as many peaches as will fit.
Top with lattice crust.
Brush crust with egg wash or milk.
Place catch pan or aluminum foil under pie in oven to catch
    drips.
Bake at 375 degrees F about 1 hour 10 minutes until crust is
    browned and peach juice is bubbling.

When peaches are in season, make this every single day—life is
short!

Spread the love, gift "Peach Pie" to friends and family.

Pie Crust

This recipe describes how to make a basic pie crust, along with several finishing techniques. This crust can be baked and then filled, according to your recipe. Your pie recipe may call for a single unbaked pie crust. Your recipe may call for adding a top crust, which may be either a solid crust or a lattice crust. If your recipe calls for adding filling to a baked crust, cool the crust completely first.

2 1/2 C white wheat flour
1 tsp salt
1/3 C salted butter
1/3 C Crisco shortening
6 to 8 T cold water
white wheat flour, for hands, table, and rolling pin

***

(option) Preheat oven to 450 degrees F.

Combine dry ingredients: flour, salt. Using two butter knives, cut in butter and shortening to dry ingredients, until crumbly. Stir in 5 T water. Stir in 1 T water. If needed, stir in more water, 1 T at a time, until dough forms into a ball. Knead gently with floured hands a few times, separating into two lumps. Form two balls.

Lightly flour the table. Place one ball on the floured surface. Liberally sprinkle the ball with flour. Roll flat with floured rolling pin, starting in the middle, pushing down, and gently pushing outward while rolling. Use more flour as needed to keep the rolling pin from sticking to the dough, and the dough from sticking to the table. Push and roll, back and forth and side to side, always starting in the middle and rolling outward to make a circle.

Pie Crust (cont.)

Roll to an even thickness, as thin as possible, but thick enough so the dough doesn't break when lifted from the table. Make the circle larger than the pie plate, large enough so that the edges will be extending over the sides of the pie plate.

Gently fold the pie crust in half over itself, and lift it up off the table, supporting it from the center. Place the folded pie crust onto one side of a glass pie plate. Unfold the crust to make a circle covering the entire pie plate. Gently ease the top edges of the crust down and into the sides of the plate.

Add the filling to the unbaked pie crust, or skip ahead to proceed to the step "Bake Unfilled." If no top crust is needed, skip ahead to "Trim."

Top Crust

Place second ball on floured surface. Roll flat. If a lattice crust is desired, skip ahead to the step "Lattice Crust."

Remove pie crust from the table. Place in pie plate over pie filling overlapping the top over the bottom crust at the edges. Gently press top crust onto bottom crust all around the edges of the pie plate. Prick top of pie crust all over with tines of a fork, to make little air holes.

Skip ahead to the step "Trim."

Lattice Crust

Slice into 1/2" wide strips. Leaving half an inch of space between strips, weave pie crust strips over filled pie, extending over edges of the pie plate. Join edges of shorter strips to fit

Pie Crust (cont.)

where needed, neatly hiding joined edges under overlapping weavings.

Trim

After filling pie and adding a top crust or lattice crust, if desired, use a butter knife to trim away the excess crust, after leaving a little bit of overhang for fluting.

Flute

On each hand, hold the thumb to the forefinger in a pinch. Flute edges by pushing down on the edge of the crust with the two sets of pinched fingers nearly side-by-side, then pushing the two sets of fingers closer together, pinching the dough into a diamond shape between the fingers. Remove the fingers from the crust, turn the pie plate a little, and make another pinched diamond. Continue to make little diamond-shaped pinches of dough all around the edge of the pie plate.

If using a baked pie crust in the recipe, make small holes in the surface of the crust before baking by pricking all over with the tines of a fork.

Bake at 450 degrees F about 8 to 10 minutes until lightly browned.

As soon as the pie crust comes out of the oven, push down the bubbles, to flatten.

Cover the pie air-tight and store it in the refrigerator to prevent the pie crust from absorbing odors or flavors.

Pumpkin Pie

1 1/2 C granulated cane sugar
1 tsp salt
2 tsp cinnamon
1 tsp ground ginger
1/2 tsp cloves
4 large eggs
1 can (29 oz) pumpkin
2 cans (12 fl oz each) evaporated milk
2 9-inch unbaked pie crusts, see recipe "Pie Crust"

***

Preheat oven to 450 degrees F.
Combine dry ingredients: sugar, salt, cinnamon, ginger, cloves.
Stir eggs together.
Stir in pumpkin and spices.
Stir in milk.
Pour into pie crusts.
Put pie into oven. Turn down oven to 425 degrees F.
Put aluminum foil or a baking sheet on the shelf below the pie
    to catch drips.
Bake 15 minutes at 425 degrees F.
Turn down oven to 375 degrees F.
Bake about 40 more minutes until a butter knife stuck into the
    center of the pie comes out clean.

Guacamole

2 avocados
1 small tomato, peeled, chopped
1 small yellow onion, minced
1 clove garlic, minced
1 tsp jalapeño, minced
1 T lemon juice
1/2 tsp salt

***

Blend together all ingredients with fork until smooth.

This is the perfect hors d'oeuvre to bring to a party, to accompany tacos, tortilla chips, "Nachos Grande," or "Quesadillas."

Nachos Grande

tortilla chips
cheddar cheese, shredded
salsa
Iceberg lettuce, shredded
1 recipe "Guacamole"
sour cream
tomato, diced
black olives, sliced
(optional) jalapeño, sliced in rounds

***

Preheat oven to 400 degrees F.
Spread tortilla chips on round baking stone.
Sprinkle liberally with cheese.
Add a second layer of tortillas and cheese.
Bake at 400 degrees F about 7 minutes, until after cheese begins
    to melt, but just before it starts bubbling.
Remove from oven.
Dot all over with salsa.
Spread lettuce evenly over center half of the dish.
Add guacamole on top, in center.
Add 2 large dollops of sour cream, one on either side of
    guacamole.
Sprinkle all over with tomatoes and black olives.
Sprinkle on a few jalapeños (optional).

Serve in the center of a table where everyone can easily reach
the dish.

Spinach Artichoke Dip

2 C grated Parmesan cheese
1 (10 oz.) box frozen chopped spinach, thawed and drained
14 oz. jar artichoke hearts, drained and chopped
2/3 C sour cream
1 C Philadelphia Cream Cheese, original
1/3 C Miracle Whip
2 tsp fresh garlic, minced
1 tsp crushed red pepper flakes

***

Mix cheese, spinach, and artichoke hearts.
Combine remaining ingredients and mix with spinach mixture.
Pour into baking dish.
Bake uncovered at 375 degrees F about 25 minutes.

Serve hot in a "Pumpernickel Bread" bowl with cubed
pumpernickel on the side for scooping up the dip.

The perfect party appetizer!

Acorn Squash Soup

2 acorn squash
water, as needed
2 T salted butter
2 large onions, chopped
2 large carrots, peeled and chopped
2 cloves garlic
2 (10.5 oz) cans chicken broth
2 oz heavy cream
1/2 tsp ground nutmeg
1/2 tsp ground cinnamon
1 pinch salt
ground pepper, to taste
water, as needed
jellied cranberry sauce, slightly warmed but not melted
small pumpkin seeds, roasted and salted (pepitas)

***

Cut squash in half and remove seeds.
Put squash halves in baking dish, flat side down.
Add water to cover the bottom of the dish.
Cover the baking dish with a lid.
Bake at 400 degrees F for 1 hour.
Scoop squash into a bowl.
In a large pot, saute the onions, carrots, and garlic in butter for 5
    to 7 minutes until soft.
Add squash and chicken broth.
Simmer 20 minutes.
Puree in blender in batches until smooth.

Heat vegetables with heavy cream, nutmeg, cinnamon, salt, and
    pepper, adding water if soup is too thick.
Add soup to individual bowls.
Swirl 2 T cranberry sauce into center of soup.
Sprinkle with seeds.

French Onion Soup

1/4 C salted butter
1 tsp granulated cane sugar
3 yellow onions
1 T flour
1/2 C red wine
2 (10.5 oz) cans beef broth
2 1/2 C water
1 French baguette, cut into 1-inch slices
(option) Mozzarella cheese
(option) Swiss cheese
(option) Brie
Parmesan cheese

***

Melt butter in 4-qt saucepan.
Stir in sugar. Add onions.
Cook at medium heat 10 minutes until onions are golden brown.
Add flour and stir well. Add wine, beef broth, and water.
Heat to boiling. Reduce heat to low. Cover. Simmer 10 minutes.
Preheat oven to 325 degrees F.
Place four 12-oz, oven-safe soup bowls on sturdy baking sheet.
Add soup to bowls.
Place 4 of the slices of French baguette on baking sheet.
Bake at 325 degrees F about 10 minutes until browned.
Preheat oven to 425 degrees F.
Top bowls of soup with 1 slice of the toasted French baguette.
Top each with a slice of cheese. Sprinkle with Parmesan cheese.
Bake at 425 degrees F about 10 minutes until cheese is melted.
Serve the rest of the French baguette slices with the soup.

Lentil Soup

3 large yellow onions
1/2 bag lentils
1 (10.5 oz) can beef broth
2 qts water
2 tsp salt
1/4 tsp pepper

***

Add all ingredients to crockpot.
Cook 4 hours, or until tender.

On Christmas Eve, it is good luck to eat as many lentils as you can. The more lentils you can eat, the more years you will live.

Split Pea Soup

1/2 bag split peas
2 qts water
3 onions
3 stalks celery
3 potatoes
6 carrots
1 (10.5 oz) can chicken broth
2 tsp salt
1/4 tsp pepper

***

Add split peas and water to crockpot.
Cook 4 hours on high until split peas are softened and cooked
through.
Run the soup through a Foley Food Mill to pulverize the
softened split peas.
Add the soup back to the crockpot.
Dice vegetables and add to crockpot and cook 2 more hours or
until tender, adding more water, if needed.

Vegetable Soup

3 large yellow onions
3 large carrots
3 stalks celery
5 potatoes
2 large tomatos or can of Redpack tomatoes
1 can pink beans or chick peas
1 (10.5 oz) can chicken or beef broth
seasonings, to taste
4 C water

***

Add all ingredients to crockpot.
Cook 4 hours, or until tender.

This is the perfect soup to use up all leftover vegetables.

Ambrosia

3/4 C sour cream
1 T granulated cane sugar
1 can (20 oz) pineapple chunks, drained
1 can (11 oz) Mandarin oranges, drained
1 banana, ripe, sliced
1 1/2 C green grapes, seedless
1 C flaked coconut
1/2 C walnuts, chopped
1 C mini-marshmallows

***

Mix sour cream and sugar.
Stir in pineapple chunks, Mandarin oranges, bananas, grapes, coconut, walnuts, and marshmallows.
Chill thoroughly. Serve cold.

Feta Walnut Cranberry Apple Salad

2 C baby spinach
2 C any baby leafy salad greens – Romaine, spring mix, lettuces
(option) 1/4 C red cabbage, thinly sliced
1/2 C feta cheese
1/2 C dried cranberries
1/2 C chopped walnuts
1 apple, thinly sliced
1 recipe "Raspberry Dressing" (optional substitution: "Marie's
    Raspberry Vinaigrette" from the refrigerated section of the
    supermarket)

***

Place each salad ingredient in its own serving bowl with serving
spoon. Serve as a "Create Your Own Salad" and provide the
dressing on the side. Add dressing just before eating.

Pasta Salad

1/2 C recipe "Salad Dressing"
16 oz pasta, bow tie or multi-color rotini
2 T olive oil
1/4 C Miracle Whip
6 green olives
2 oz pepper jack cheese
1 tomato
1 stalk celery
1 carrot
1 cucumber
1/2 red bell pepper
1/2 green bell pepper
1 T diced onion
1 tsp salt
1 tsp parsley
1/4 tsp pepper
1/4 tsp oregano
1/8 tsp rosemary

***

Cook pasta to al dente and drain thoroughly.
Add olive oil to pasta and stir to coat.
Dice cheese, olives, and vegetables.
Gently stir together all ingredients until evenly mixed.
Chill until serving.

Sugared Almond Salad

1/4 C almonds, slivered, blanched
2 T granulated cane sugar
1/2 head iceberg lettuce
1/2 head Romaine lettuce
1 scallion, sliced in rounds, both white and green
1 stalk celery, sliced thinly
1 (10 oz) can Mandarin oranges, drained
1 recipe "Tangy Dressing"

***

Spread almonds on frying pan over medium to low heat.
Sprinkle sugar over almonds.
Heat slowly, stirring constantly, until sugar melts and almonds
turn golden brown.
Remove to a plate, to cool.
Shred lettuce into bite-sized pieces.
Add scallions, celery, and Mandarin oranges.
Spread almonds on top.
Toss salad, adding "Tangy Dressing" at the last minute.
Eat salad immediately.

Tuna Pasta Salad

1 recipe "Tuna Fish Salad"
16 oz pasta, bow tie or elbow
2 T olive oil
1 stalk celery
1 cucumber
1/2 green bell pepper
1/4 C Miracle Whip
1 T diced yellow onion
1 tsp salt
1 tsp parsley
1/4 tsp oregano
1/8 tsp pepper

***

Cook pasta to al dente and drain thoroughly.
Add olive oil to pasta and stir to coat.
Dice vegetables.
Gently stir together all ingredients until evenly mixed.
Chill until serving.

Raspberry Dressing

6 T olive oil
6 T raspberry vinegar
1 tsp fresh lemon juice
1/2 tsp sugar

***

Combine all ingredients.
Whisk to blend well.

Serve with "Feta Walnut Cranberry Apple Salad."
Add dressing at the last minute, just before eating.

Salad Dressing

1 C vinegar
1/4 C olive oil
1 tsp lemon juice
1 tsp sugar
1/2 tsp parsley
1/8 tsp oregano
1 pinch salt
1 shake pepper

***

Combine all ingredients.
Whisk to blend well.

Tangy Dressing

1/4 C olive oil
2 T sugar
2 T vinegar
1 T parsley, dried
1/2 tsp salt
dash pepper
dash red pepper sauce

***

Combine all ingredients.
Whisk to blend well.

This salad dressing is especially good on the salad recipe
"Sugared Almond Salad."

Vinaigrette

4 T red wine vinegar
1 T Dijon mustard
1 tsp sugar
1/2 tsp salt
minced parsley
fresh snipped chives
1/2 C olive oil

***

Whisk together red wine vinegar, Dijon mustard, sugar, salt, parsley, and chives.
Continue whisking while drizzling in the olive oil.
Continue whisking until thickened.

This is the perfect dressing for a Nicoise Salad or a green leafy salad with tomatoes, carrots, and cucumbers.

Cornmeal Mush

water
corn meal
salt
whole milk
granulated cane sugar

***

Measure ingredients according to package directions for hot
wheat cereal, substituting corn meal for the wheat, for as
many as are expected to show up for breakfast. Double the
amount of water.
Mix water, corn meal, and salt in saucepan.
Cook on high 1 minute. Lower to simmer.
Cook 10 minutes. Add milk.
Cook 4 minutes. Turn off heat.
Stir in sugar.

Serve in individual bowls, with a bowl of sugar and a small
pitcher of warm milk on the side.

Eggs Benedict

1/2 English muffin, toasted
1 tsp salted butter
2 slices crisp bacon (optional, substitute slice of ham)
1 large egg, recipe "Poached Eggs"
2 T recipe "Hollandaise Sauce"

***

Spread butter on non-flat side of muffin.
Place muffin on plate, flat side down.
Top muffin with bacon (or ham), egg, and "Hollandaise Sauce."

Make "Hollandaise Sauce" and serve the recipe "Eggs Benedict" for a delicious fancy breakfast or brunch.

Granola

2 C rolled oats
1/2 C walnuts, chopped
1 tsp cinnamon
1/3 C honey
1/3 C dark brown sugar
1/4 C vegetable oil
1 1/2 tsp pure vanilla extract
1/2 C dried cherries
1/2 C sunflower seeds

***

Mix: honey, brown sugar, oil.
Simmer over low heat until thick.
Remove from heat.
Stir in vanilla.
Pour syrup over dry ingredients.
Toss to coat.
Spread on parchment-lined baking sheet.
Bake at 300 degrees F about 30 minutes until.granola is crispy
    and begins to brown.
Cool slightly.
Stir in fruit and seeds.
Serve this cereal in a bowl with milk.

Hot Cereal

water
wheat grain cereal
salt
whole milk
granulated cane sugar

***

Measure ingredients according to package directions, for as
    many people as are expected to show up for breakfast.
Mix water, wheat cereal, and salt in saucepan.
Cook on high 1 minute. Lower to simmer.
Cook 6 minutes. Add milk.
Cook 4 minutes. Turn off heat.
Stir in sugar.
Serve with warm milk and sugar on the side.

Oatmeal

1 C water
1 C Quaker original oatmeal
1 C whole milk
1/8 tsp salt
1 apple, diced
1 T granulated cane sugar

***

Mix in saucepan: water, oatmeal, milk, salt, apple.
Cook on high 1 minute. Lower to simmer.
Cook 5 minutes. Turn off heat.
Stir in 1 T sugar.

Pancakes

1 1/4 C white wheat flour
2 T granulated cane sugar
2 tsp baking powder
1 large egg
1 T vegetable oil
1 C whole milk, plus more, if needed
chocolate chips
chocolate syrup
blueberries, fresh or frozen
pears, peeled, very ripe, slightly mashed
fresh strawberries, sliced
chocolate chips
sliced bananas, apples, or peaches
sliced cantaloupe or watermelon
fresh blueberries, raspberries, or strawberries
walnuts, chopped into tiny pieces
chocolate syrup
real maple syrup
honey
grape jelly
salted butter
sour cream
1 recipe:"Whipped Cream"

***

Combine dry ingredients: flour, sugar, baking powder.
Combine wet ingredients: egg, oil, milk.
Add dry ingredients to wet ingredients and stir just to combine.
    Don't over stir.
If too thick, add more milk.
To customize, take orders in advance from each person as to
    preferred size, fillings, and toppings for each pancake.

>>

Pancakes (cont.)

For a Blueberry, Pear, or Chocolate Pancake, fill the ladle with batter, then stir in 2 T of blueberries or mashed pears or 1 tsp chocolate syrup.

Ladle batter, all at once, onto a hot pancake griddle, so it forms an even circle.

For regular pancakes, make 4-inch circles.

For smaller pancakes, thin the batter slightly by adding a little more milk.

For Mini Pancakes, make 2-inch circles.

For Polka Dot Pancakes, make each circle under an inch in diameter.

For Chocolate Chip Pancakes, add a sprinkling of chocolate chips on top of each pancake while cooking before flipping.

Watch the pancake as it cooks. When lots of little air bubbles form at the edges of the pancake and the center starts to almost solidify, peek at the underside by lifting the edge of the pancake with a spatula.

When the reverse side is properly browned, flip the pancake over with the spatula and cook the other side until also browned.

Add toppings to each pancake, to taste. Serve hot.

Top pancakes with any combination of butter, real maple syrup, honey, jelly, fresh fruits, whipped cream, or sour cream.

Turn any morning into a party! Custom make each person's pancake by adding a little extra something to each ladle of batter, either chocolate chips or bits of fruit.

Make pancakes of all sizes, including teeny Polka Dot Pancakes. Enjoy a variety of delicious and nutritious toppings.

Great for the kids for sleepovers!

Pancakes (cont.)

For the ultimate party breakfast, serve with a variety of foods that go great with pancakes: bacon, scrambled eggs, cantaloupe, home fries, OJ.

Leftover plain pancakes are even great cold. Spread with grape jelly and roll into a jelly roll. Great for long car trips or as a sweet treat included in a bagged lunch.

Poached Eggs

water, to fill saucepan to 3 inches deep
2 large eggs
salt and pepper, to taste

***

Heat water in pan to simmering.
Carefully break each egg into a small dish without breaking the
    yolk.
Slide each egg into the simmering water.
Simmer about 3 minutes, until the egg is cooked.
Remove eggs from pan, one at a time, with a slotted spoon to
    drain out the water.
Place egg onto toast or English muffin.
Season with salt and pepper, to taste.

"Poached Eggs" may be served on toast or English muffins or
used as an ingredient in "Eggs Benedict."

Waffles

1 3/4 C white wheat flour
1 T baking powder
1 3/4 C whole milk
1/2 C vegetable oil
2 large egg yolks
2 large egg whites, beaten until fluffy
salted butter, for topping
confectioner's sugar, for topping
real maple syrup, for topping
honey, for topping
grape jelly, for topping
fresh strawberries, for topping
1 recipe: "Whipped Cream," for topping

***

Preheat waffle iron.
Mix: milk, oil, yolks.
Add dry ingredients and beat well.
Gently fold in the fluffy egg whites.
Drop, all at once, one ladle of batter onto hot waffle iron.
Cook until crisp.
Serve with toppings, as desired.

Make waffles fresh for each person as they arrive for breakfast!

If you know everyone in your household is going to be waking up leisurely at different times, this is the perfect "easy but delicious" treat for breakfast. Just make the batter, and then turn on the waffle iron to preheat when you hear footsteps.

Mac-N-Cheese

mozzarella cheese, diced
pepper Jack cheese, diced
Swiss cheese, diced
cream cheese, diced
16 oz elbow macaroni, cooked to just before al dente, drained
8 oz cheddar cheese, shredded
2 C cottage cheese
1 C sour cream
1 tsp salt
1/4 tsp pepper
whole milk (optional)
2 T Parmesan cheese, for topping
1 oz cheddar cheese, shredded, for topping
breadcrumbs (optional) , for topping
1/2 tsp paprika (optional), for topping

***

Select any combination of cheeses to add to this dish. Feel free
to use up any leftover cheese from your refrigerator.
In a large casserole dish, stir together: diced cheeses, macaroni,
cheddar cheese, cottage cheese, sour cream, salt, pepper.
Add a little milk (optional), if desired.
Sprinkle top with Parmesan cheese, cheddar cheese, bread
crumbs (optional), and paprika.
Bake at 350 degrees F, uncovered, about 30 minutes.

Sesame Noodles

water, for boiling chicken
salt, to taste
2 cloves garlic, cut
4 thin slices ginger, fresh
1/2 lb chicken cutlets
6 T peanut butter
5 T soy sauce
1 1/2 T sugar
1 T warm water
1 T sesame oil
1 T rice vinegar
1/4 C ginger, fresh, minced
4 cloves garlic, minced
1/2 lb linguini, cooked
1 T sesame oil
10 snow peas, slivered
1/2 cucumber, cut in slivers
1/2 red bell pepper, diced
1 C bean sprouts

***

Simmer in water: salt, garlic, ginger, and chicken, until chicken
    is cooked.
Chop chicken to shreds.
Blend in blender until smooth: peanut butter, soy sauce, sugar,
    water, sesame oil, rice vinegar, ginger, garlic.
Toss linguini with sesame oil and chopped chicken.
Add sauce.
Top with snow peas, cucumber, red bell peppers, bean sprouts.
Serve immediately, with chopsticks.

Spaghetti

Ronzoni or Barilla wheat pasta, any shape or size
Prego Sauce, mushroom or any flavor
meatballs or browned ground meat (optional)
Parmesan cheese (optional) , for topping

***

Cook spaghetti in boiling water according to package directions.
While spaghetti is cooking, heat pasta sauce.
Combine and serve hot.

Baked Beans

3 (16 oz) cans prepared baked beans
1/2 C Heinz tomato ketchup
1/2 C brown sugar
1 T Grandma's Molasses
1 tsp mustard
1 small yellow onion, minced
2 slices bacon, cooked crisp, chopped (optional)

***

Mix together: baked beans, ketchup, brown sugar, molasses, mustard, onion, and (optional) bacon.
Pour into 2-qt baking dish. Cover.
Bake at 350 degrees F about 1 hour.

Baked Potatoes

6 baking potatoes

***

Scrub the skins.
Pierce with fork all over, to allow release of steam in baking.
Bake at 400 degrees F about 1 hour 20 minutes.

Serve plain or with butter and salt or sour cream.

Refrigerate leftovers to eat plain or sliced and fried in butter until crispy on both sides.

Baked Yams or Sweet Potatoes

6 yams or sweet potatoes

***

Scrub the skins.
Pierce with fork all over, to allow release of steam in baking.
Bake at 400 degrees F about 1 hour 10 minutes.

Busy Dieter's Dream

Busy schedule? Plan ahead. Keep frozen mixed vegetables in the freezer in a container easy to reseal, like a Ziploc Freezer Bag. Make up to a week before and keep in the refrigerator peeled carrots, peeled hard-boiled "Boiled Eggs," and"Baked Potatoes." Keep fresh apples on the counter in an open bowl lined with a cotton cloth, or, if insects are a problem in the house, keep them in a cloth bag in the refrigerator crisper drawer.

The apples, that is, not the insects. You can keep apples in the refrigerator. Though refrigerated apples will develop a mealy consistency, the apples will still be nutritious.

Don't be so picky. This dish is not for picky eaters.

2 T water
1 C frozen mixed vegetables
1 peeled hard-boiled egg
1 baked potato (can be eaten cold or warmed in microwave)
1 peeled carrot
1 apple, washed and dried
glass of tap water to drink (can be warmed in microwave)

***

Add tap water to microwaveable glass bowl.
Add mixed veggies.
Cover bowl with glass plate that overlaps edge of bowl.
Nuke 3 minutes until hot. Drain.

Serve hot mixed veggies with a hard-boiled egg, a plain baked potato, and water to drink, with an apple for dessert.

Ambrosia for the gods! where the gods work sixteen-hour shifts and don't want to load up on fast food and ruin their health.

Candied Carrots

1 lb carrots, sliced into rounds
water, for boiling
1/4 C orange juice
2 T salted butter
3 T brown sugar
1 pinch salt

***

Add carrots to sauce pan.
Add water, to cover carrots.
Boil until tender, then drain.
Simmer the cooked carrots in the orange juice for 5 minutes.
Add the butter, brown sugar, and salt.
Heat, stirring, until melted.

Carrots and Celery Platter

6 carrots
6 stalks celery
1 cucumber
1 zucchini
1 green bell pepper, seeded
1 yellow bell pepper, seeded
1 red bell pepper, seeded

***

Scrub the skins.
Slice into 2" strips.

Celeriac

1 small celeriac, diced into small pieces
water, for boiling

***

Add celeriac to sauce pan.
Add water, to cover.
Boil until tender, then drain.

A seasonal root vegetable with an unusual earthy flavor; smells like celery, potato-like consistency, interesting aftertaste.

Add to tuna, egg, or potato salad, pasta sauce, or soup.

Gruel

1 can Progresso Lentil Soup
1 can black beans
1 can kidney beans
1 can chick peas
barley
spinach
kale
bell peppers
zucchini
carrots
celery
onions

***

Combine all ingredients.
Add any other vegetable, bean, or legume.
Bring to a boil.
Package into single-meal servings.
Freeze.
Heat and eat one when hungry.

My sister made up this recipe and followed it faithfully. It kept
her alive all during medial school and law school and saved her
a lot of time.

Kohlrabi

kohlrabi

***

Peel off the hard skin and then also cut off the outer layer, which is tough and fibrous.
Cut kohlrabi into strips like French fries.
Bake like French fries.

Latkes

6 baking potatoes
1 onion, minced
1 large egg, beaten
2 tsp salt
1/8 tsp pepper
1/2 C oil
1 C sour cream
2 C applesauce

***

Grate the potatoes into strips, placing immediately into a bowl
of ice-cold water to help keep them from turning brown.
Soak the grated potatoes for 3 minutes.
Retaining the water in the bowl, use a slotted spoon to remove
the potatoes to a cotton cloth kitchen towel.
Press the potatoes in the towel to remove as much moisture as
possible.
Allow the potato water to sit for ten minutes, so the potato
starch will sink to the bottom of the bowl.
Pour the top liquid off the potato water, retaining the potato
starch.
Mix together the potato starch, potatoes, onions, egg, salt, and
pepper.
Heat the oil in a cast iron skillet.
Cook latkes in batches of 4.
Use 2 T of the potato mixture for each latke, forming by hand
into flattened pancakes, and add in a single layer to the hot
oil.
Fry on one side about 5 minutes until golden brown on the
bottom, then turn and fry on the other side.
Remove latkes from skillet using slotted spoon, and drain
cooked latkes on paper towels.
Serve hot, with sour cream and applesauce on the side.

Latkes (cont.)

Latkes may be kept warm in oven set at 250 degrees F.
Refrigerate leftovers.

To reheat later, place on cookie sheet and bake at 350 degrees F
about 5 minutes.

Mashed Potatoes

12 white potatoes

***

Scrub the skins.
Cut into 2" chunks.
Boil until tender, until fork easily pierces the skin.
Allow to cool slightly until comfortable to the touch. Scrape off
    skin and cut out rough spots.
Keep plain or add to taste: sour cream, butter, salt.
Mix with electric mixer in metal bowl until light and fluffy.
Fluff up with a spatula to form peaks on top.
Bake at 400 degrees F until peaks brown.

Serve plain or with butter and salt or sour cream.

Open-Faced Radish and Scallion Sandwiches

6 red radishes
seeded Russian rye bread
salted butter
scallions, trimmed and sliced into rounds

***

Scrub the radish skins.
Cut into thin slices.
Lay in a single layer on lightly buttered rye.
Top with scallion rounds.

These open-faced sandwiches are best using fresh bread and
radishes just picked from the garden.

Sushi

1 C rice vinegar
3/8 C granulated cane sugar
2 T salt, plus a pinch
1 piece nori (paper-thin sheets of kelp), 3 inches square
2 1/2 C water
pinch salt
2 C rice
1 tsp sake (optional)
pickled mustard greens, for filling
scallions, for filling
cucumber, for filling
Japanese radish, for filling
pressed tofu, for filling
bean sprouts, for filling
flavorful meat or sausage, for filling
fish or shellfish, cooked, for filling
eggs, scrambled, cooked as a thin, flat pancake, for filling
water, to moisten nori

***

Combine rice vinegar, sugar, and salt.
Shake or stir until dissolved.
Add nori. Let sit 30 minutes.
Remove nori.
Cover container.
Let sit 2 hours, up to 2 days, at or below room temperature.
Cook water salt, rice, and sake (optional) in rice cooker.
Let cool 15 minutes.
Fold in about 1/2 C of the vinegar, a little at a time, until rice is
    glistening, but not wet.
Choose fillings, from among those on the list. Use a variety of
    colors and flavors. Include at least 2 of the vegetables, with
    or without eggs and/or one of the meats or fishes.

>>

Sushi (cont.)

Cut fillings into very thin strips.

Lay a single sheet of nori flat on the table.

Spread rice thinly, about 1/4", onto a single sheet of nori. (This is not easy, as rice will be sticky.) Starting at the bottom edge, cover almost the entire sheet, leaving uncovered a blank strip 1" wide at the top edge.

Lay a thin, neat row, of one of the fillings, on top of the rice, placed about half an inch from the bottom edge.

Make layers, a thin row of each of the fillings, atop the first filling.

Using a brush, moisten the top 1-inch edge of the nori along its entire length.

Pick up the bottom edge of the nori and push its entire length firmly up onto the pile of ingredients. Continue to roll up from the bottom edge, rolling it all up, to form a tight cylinder.

Press down firmly, for the length of the edge, on the moistened nori, to seal the seam.

Slice into 1-in rolls.

Place sushi rolls, cut side up, onto serving platter.

Serve with a little side dish of soy sauce, for dipping.

Texas Caviar

1 bag Tostitos Multi-Grain Scoops
1 can sweet corn
2 cans black beans, rinsed and drained
1 can black eyed peas, rinsed and drained
1-2 small jars pimientos, diced
1 medium red onion, minced
1 C apple cider vinegar
1 C granulated cane sugar
1 C olive oil

***

Combine: corn, beans, peas, pimientos, onion.
In a sauce pan, combine:vinegar, sugar, oil:
Bring to a boil.
Pour liquid over combined corn, beans etc.
Refrigerate overnight.
In the morning, drain extra liquid and enjoy.

Serve with Tostitos Multi Grain Scoops.

Chicken Marinade

1/2 C hoisin sauce
1/4 C soy sauce
3 T dry sherry
1/2 tsp mustard
1 T brown sugar
1 tsp ground ginger
2 scallions, finely chopped

***

Mix together all ingredients.

Lime Chicken Marinade

1 C water
1/3 C teriyaki sauce
1/2 lime, fresh, juice only
3 cloves garlic
1/2 tsp salt
1/4 tsp ground ginger

***

Mix together all ingredients.

Salmon Marinade

1/3 C orange juice
1/3 C soy sauce
3 T ketchup
3 T oil
1 T honey
1/2 tsp ginger, ground

***

Mix together all ingredients.

Sesame Chicken Marinade

2 T white wheat flour
1/4 tsp baking soda
1/4 tsp baking powder
2 T corn starch
2 T water
2 T soy sauce
1 T dry sherry
1 tsp oil
3 drops sesame oil

***

Combine dry ingredients: flour, baking soda, baking powder, corn starch.
Combine wet ingredients: water, soy sauce, sherry, oils.
Add wet ingredients to dry ingredients.
Whisk to stir well.

Salmon

salmon steak or filet with skin on
1 recipe "Salmon Marinade," optional
3 cloves garlic, sliced, optional
1/2 lemon, sliced into rounds, seeded, optional

***

Butter a glass pie plate or baking dish large enough to lay out
    the salmon flat.
Place salmon skin-side down in dish.
Option 1
    no added ingredients.
Option 2
    Add "Salmon Marinade" and marinate in refrigerator one
    hour.
Option 3:
    Sprinkle salmon with garlic.
    Arrange lemon slices to cover surface of salmon.
Bake at 400 degrees F for 15 to 20 minutes.

Salt Fish

water, for boiling
salt fish (cod)
1 recipe "Fry Bread for Salt Fish"

***

Soak the salt fish in a pot of water overnight, to remove most of
the salt.
If it is still very salty, boil in water for 20 minutes.
Drain well and press dry in kitchen towel.
Cut or tear into small pieces.
Heat in frying pan.
Serve with "Fry Bread for Salt Fish."

A simple and delicious way to serve salt fish, to be scooped up
with bite-sized pieces of fry bread.

Shrimp Creole

1 T vegetable oil
1 C onion
1/2 T celery
1/2 C bell pepper
6 cloves garlic
1 (14.5 oz) can diced tomatoes
2 tomatoes
1 bay leaves
1 T sugar
1 tsp salt
1/2 tsp pepper
1 lb shrimp
2 T flour
1 C water

***

Add all ingredients to crock pot.
Cook until tender.
Serve over cooked brown rice.

Tuna Fish Salad

1 large can tuna, solid Albacore packed in water
3 T Miracle Whip
3 T pickle relish, drained
2 T finely chopped celery
1 tsp minced onion
1/2 tsp parsley
1/4 tsp Gulden's spicy brown mustard
1/4 tsp celery seed
1/8 tsp oregano
1/4 tsp salt
2 dashes pepper

***

Drain the water from the tuna fish, pressing out as much of the liquid as possible.
Add all ingredients and stir together with a large spoon until evenly textured and thoroughly combined. You may need to repeatedly mash flat the tuna fish chunks against the side of the bowl to break them apart.

"Tuna Fish Salad" is great on hard rolls or on whole wheat toast with lettuce and tomato and a little mayonnaise.

It may also be mixed in with cooked pasta and extra mayonnaise to make a Tuna Pasta Salad.

All by itself, it is a great side dish at a barbecue or accompanying a green salad for brunch.

Boiled Eggs

water
6 eggs

***

Place eggs in sauce pan with water to cover.
Bring to a boil slowly, so the eggs won't crack. Keep the
temperature at boiling, just above a simmer, but not at a
roiling boil.

Soft-Boiled Eggs

Boil 3 minutes. Start timing from the first boiling bubble.
Rinse in cold water immediately, to release the egg from its
shell.
Holding the egg on end in your hand, carefully use a spoon to
crack the shell at its middle. Turning the egg, make cracks
all the way around.
Slide the spoon into the egg at its mid-point, and pull the top
half off. Allow the runny part to fall into the egg cup. Be
sure to retrieve all bits of shell immediately before they get
mixed into the runny part.
Holding one half the egg, insert the bowl of the spoon between
the shell and the egg and push bown, to dig along the edge
of the inside of the shell and get the spoon under the egg at
the bottom. Turn the egg upside down, to release the half of
the egg from the shell.
Repeat with the other half of the egg.
Use the spoon to chop the hard whites into smaller bits to mix
with the yellow runny part.

Hard-Boiled Eggs

Boil five minutes. Cover pot, turn off heat. Let stand ten
minutes. Run under cold water. Crack shell by hitting on
table and rolling under palm. Remove shell bits.

Chicken Cranberry Salad

4 C chicken, poached, diced
1 C celery, diced small
1 C pecans
1 C dried cranberries
1 1/2 C white seedless grapes quartered
1 C white raisins
4 oz sour cream
1 C Miracle Whip
to taste: salt, pepper

***

Mix salad ingredients.

Chicken, Rice, and Peas

1 recipe "White Sauce" (optional substitution: 1 can Campbell's
    Cream of Chicken Soup)
3 C whole milk
1 lb cooked chicken, chopped into bite-sized pieces
3 C cooked brown rice
4 C frozen peas
2 large "Boiled Eggs," hard-boiled, sliced into 1/4" slices
paprika

***

Heat "White Sauce" (or soup) with milk. Add chicken.

Stir in rice, then peas.

Spread in casserole dish.

Arrange egg slices on top of casserole to decorate.

Sprinkle with paprika.

Bake at 375 degrees F about 1 hour.

Half-way into the cooking, cover to keep eggs from drying out.

Egg Whites

The secret for beating egg whites into peaks is to use cold and dry and extremely clean beaters, bowl, and spatula.

Lime Chicken

1 recipe "Lime Chicken Marinade"
chicken breasts, skinless, boneless, flattened
1/4 C sour cream
1/4 C Miracle Whip
2 T salsa
1 T whole milk
1 tsp Cajun blackening spice
1/4 tsp parsley
1/4 tsp hot sauce
1/8 tsp cumin
1/8 tsp dill
Colby Jack cheese, shredded
cheddar cheese, shredded

***

Marinate chicken in "Lime Chicken Marinade" in refrigerator
    for 2 hours.
Grill chicken on barbecue until cooked.
Preheat oven to 400 degrees F.
Combine dressing: sour cream, Miracle Whip, salsa, milk,
    Cajun spice, parsley, hot sauce, cumin, dill.
Brush chicken with dressing.
Sprinkle chicken with cheeses to cover.
Broil at 400 degrees F about 4 to 5 minutes, or just until cheeses
    melt.

Marinated Chicken

1 recipe "Chicken Marinade"
2 lbs chicken pieces

***

Marinate chicken in refrigerator 2 hours.
Grill chicken on barbecue until cooked.

Quesadillas

1 recipe "Guacamole
chicken, cooked, cut to bite-sized
salsa
iceberg lettuce, shredded
sour cream
tomato, diced
black olives, sliced
(optional) jalapeño, sliced in rounds, for topping
soft flour or corn tortillas
cheddar cheese, shredded, for filling
cooked chicken, shredded, for filling
refried beans, for filling

***

Put each in its own serving bowl with spoon: "Guacamole,"
    chicken, salsa, lettuce, sour cream, tomato, jalapeño,
    cheeses.
Preheat electric Quesadilla Maker until the Ready Light comes
    on.
Open the lid of the Quesadilla Maker.
Place one tortilla in the center of the Quesadilla Maker.
Sprinkle tortilla liberally with cheese and chicken.
Add a second tortilla on top.
Lower the lid of the Quesadilla Maker.
Cook until the Ready Light comes on.
Remove each quesadilla to an individual plate as it is finished.
Serve immediately with "Guacamole" and other toppings on the
    side.

Individual quesadillas are fun to make with the Quesadilla
Maker, and each person adds their own favorite toppings.

Sesame Chicken

1 recipe "Sesame Chicken Marinade"
chicken
1 C chicken broth
1/4 C rice wine vinegar
2 T dark soy sauce
2 T sesame oil
1 tsp chili paste
2 T corn starch
1/2 C water
1 C granulated cane sugar
vegetable oil, for frying

***

Marinate chicken 20 minutes in the refrigerator.
In saucepan, heat on medium: chicken broth, vinegar, soy sauce,
    sesame oil, chili paste.
In a small lidded jar, shake cornstarch with water to make a
    slurry.
Stir slurry and sugar into sauce. Bring to a boil.
Simmer 5 minutes or until sauce is thickened.
Deep fry chicken in oil.
Coat chicken with sauce.

Serve over a bed of hot, fluffy brown rice with a side of stir-
fried vegetables.

Taco Bake

1 block of sharp cheddar cheese
1 pkg soft flour or corn tortillas
1 C cooked chicken, cut into bite-sized chunks
1 can Campbell's Cream of Mushroom Soup
1 can Campbell's Cream of Chicken Soup
1 large onion, diced
1 large bell pepper, diced
1 can chilis, chopped
1 can chick peas, drained

***

Cut slices of cheese enough to be able to create a layer to top the finished dish. Reserve slices.

Shred the rest of the cheese.

Line a large, very deep baking dish with tortillas to cover the entire bottom and sides. They will overlap.

Split into three equal portions the layering ingredients: chicken, cream of mushroom soup, cream of chicken soup, onion, bell pepper, chilis, chick peas, shredded cheese. No mixing of ingredients is required. Do not reconstitute the soups.

Make each of the three casserole layers the same. Spread each of the ingredients over the layer, then add a layer of tortillas.

Flatten the top layer, then top the dish with a layer of cheddar cheese slices. Be careful not to let the tortillas stick up past the top layer of cheese or they will burn.

Cover and bake at 375 degrees F for about 50 minutes or until thoroughly heated.

With ten minutes left to bake, take off the lid to check the consistency. If it looks too soupy, leave the lid off. If it is dry enough, put the lid back on. Finish baking.

This recipe is very flexible. Use more or less of anything. Substitutions are fine.

Reheat leftovers in the oven in single servings, covered, at 350 degrees F for about 20 minutes or until heated through.

Turkey, Gravy and Stuffing

fresh 24 lb Pepperidge Farm Tom turkey
uncooked turkey giblets, except liver, from packet inside fresh
    turkey, rinsed
water for boiling turkey giblets, more as needed for gravy
2 T salted butter
1 large yellow onion, diced, for giblet water
2 stalks celery, diced, for giblet water
1 large carrot, diced, for giblet water
6 cloves garlic, sliced, for giblet water
1 pkg Pepperidge Farm seasoned cubed stuffing (or use your
own cubed stale bread)
salted butter, salt, pepper, poultry seasoning, tarragon, parsley,
    rosemary, for stuffing
1 large yellow onion, chopped, for stuffing
2 stalks celery, diced, , for stuffing
1 large carrot, diced, for stuffing
1 C walnuts, chopped, for stuffing
1 C fresh cranberries, chopped, for stuffing
salted butter, salt, pepper, for turkey skin
1 tsp tarragon, for turkey skin
1/4 tsp paprika, for turkey skin
1/4 tsp cayenne pepper, for turkey skin
1/2 C 4C seasoned bread crumbs, for turkey skin
to taste: poultry seasoning, salt, pepper, tarragon, parsley, for
    gravy

***

Before cooking turkey, boil turkey giblets in water until cooked.
    Reserve cooking water.
Cut giblets into tiny pieces; reserve meat and discard bones or
    gristle.
Add butter and onions to large cooking pot. Saute onion 3
    minutes or until fragrant.

>>

Turkey, Gravy and Stuffing (cont.)

Add celery and carrots. Stir. Cook two more minutes.

Stir in: garlic, giblets, 1C turkey giblet water. Bring to a boil.

Make Pepperidge Farm Stuffing according to package
directions, measuring the giblet water for liquid. If using
your own cubed stale bread (white, wheat, rye, with or
without seeds), flavor with butter and herbs; spread on
baking sheet in oven; bake at 350 degree F until toasted,
turning frequently.

Reserve and refrigerate the rest of the giblet water, for gravy.

Add to the stuffing: onions, celery, carrots, walnuts, cranberries.
Stuff turkey. Place on raised rack in roasting pan. Rub skin
with: oil, salt, pepper, garlic, poultry seasoning, paprika,
cayenne pepper. Sprinkle with bread crumbs, to cover.

Roast turkey according to package instructions.

After two hours, tent with aluminum foil to keep skin from
burning.

After two more hours, or when skin is crisped, remove tent, and
cover roasting pan with lid to prevent turkey from drying
out.

Remove turkey from roasting pan.

Add 1 C water to roasting pan and stir to release stuck bits into
turkey drippings.

Add turkey drippings and bits to pot with onions and giblets for
gravy.

Add, to taste: poultry seasoning, salt, pepper, tarragon, parsley.

Serve with cranberry sauce, mashed potatoes, baked yams,
"Ambrosia," "Sesame Seed Bread," brie cheese, "Cornbread,"
green bean casserole, "Sugar Almond Salad," corn on the cob,
"Baked Beans," "Zucchini Bread," "Pumpkin Pie," red wine,
coffee, cognac. Bring to the table your hopes and dreams for the
future to share with the other guests. Listen when they talk.
Allow them to speak their minds. Don't judge. Let it go. Smile.

Beef Stew

2 T vegetable oil
1 lb beef cubes
3 large yellow onions, sliced
2 bell peppers, sliced
3 carrots, sliced in rounds
3 stalks celery, sliced in rounds
5 potatoes, sliced in large cubes
6 cloves garlic, diced
1 can chick peas
2 large cans of tomatoes in puree
1 tsp parsley
1/2 tsp basil
1/4 tsp oregano
1/8 tsp rosemary
1 tsp salt
1/4 tsp pepper
1 C peas, frozen
1 C corn, frozen

***

Brown the meat in oil in a frying pan or cast iron skillet.
Add meat and all ingredients except peas and corn to crockpot.
Cook 4 hours, or until tender.
Add peas and corn and cook five more minutes until tender.
You can add your leftover veggies to this stew.
Serve with brown rice or bread and butter and red wine.

Chili

2 T olive oil
2 T soybean oil
1 lb beef cubes
3 yellow onions, sliced
3 bell peppers, sliced
1 large can of Redpack tomatoes with puree and herbs
1 large can of Redpack plum tomatoes
1 can Campbell's Tomato Soup
1 tsp salt
1/4 tsp pepper
2 tsp parsley
1 tsp basil
1/4 tsp oregano
1/4 tsp rosemary
2 tsp chili powder
1 can chick peas
1 can black beans
1 can pinto beans
2 tsp granulatedd cane sugar

***

Heat 2 T olive oil in crock pot on high.
While the oil is heating, stir fry the beef cubes in 2 T oil in a
    cast iron pot, browning thoroughly on all sides.
Cover and continue to cook on medium.
Stir in onions and cook five minutes, stirring occasionally.
Stir in peppers and cook five minutes, stirring occasionally.
Add cooked beef stew meat to crock pot, stirring into the
    vegetables.
Add the rest of the ingredients except beans and sugar.
Stir the spices into the liquid at the top.
Add beans and sugar and stir gently.
Cook 4 hours, until vegetables are soft and flavors are blended.
Serve plain or over brown rice or baked potatoes or in tacos or
    on "Nachos Grande."

Ham with Pineapple Slices

1 ham steak
2 T brown sugar
2 T salted butter
1 can Dole pineapple slices in juice

***

Place butter in frying pan.
Arrange ham in frying pan.
Sear on both sides to get a little crisp.
Sprinkle with brown sugar.
Arrange pineapple slices over ham.
Pour 1/2 C pineapple juice over ham.
Cook until hot.

Kielbasa

2 T vegetable oil
1 kielbasa sausage, cut into 1/4 inch rounds

***

Heat oil in cast iron skillet with raised sides.
Fry each kielbasa, turning, until thoroughly heated and crispy
  on both sides.

Meatball Subs

2 lb ground beef, 85% lean
1/4 C Heinz tomato ketchup
1/4 C 4C seasoned bread crumbs
1 tsp salt
1/4 tsp pepper
1 large egg
1/4 C onion, minced
1/8 C bell pepper, diced
vegetable oil, for browning meatballs
2 T olive oil
2 yellow onions, diced
1 bell pepper, diced
1 small can tomato paste with Italian seasonings
1 jar spaghetti sauce, Prego Traditional
long sub rolls, sliced open lengthwise, but not all the way
    through

***

Mix ground beef, ketchup, bread crumbs, salt, pepper, egg,
    onions, and bell peppers.
Make 2-in meatballs.
Spread 2 T oil in cast iron pan.
Heat until hot.
Add meatballs to pan in a single layer.
Cook over medium-high heat until browned on all sides,
    occasionally stirring gently to turn.
Remove meatballs from pan.
Repeat, browning the remaining meatballs.
Turn crockpot on high.
Add olive oil and heat 5 minutes.
Stir in onions. Cook 15 minutes. Add bell peppers.
Stir in: garlic, spaghetti sauce, tomato paste, meatballs.
Cook 4 hours or until done.
Ladle meatballs, single file, along center of open sub roll.
Cover meatballs with sauce.

Meatloaf

1 to 2 lb mix of ground beef, pork, and lamb
1 large egg, slightly beaten
1 can chick peas
1/2 C V-8 Spicy Hot vegetable juice
1/4 C Heinz ketchup
1 yellow onion, minced
1/4 C 4C seasoned bread crumbs
1 T parsley, dried
1/2 tsp basil, dried
1/8 tsp oregano, dried
1 tsp salt
1/8 tsp pepper
1/2 C Prego mushroom spaghetti sauce, for topping

***

Gently mix meatloaf ingredients: meats, egg, chick peas, juice, ketchup, onion, bread crumbs, parsley, basil, oregano, salt, pepper.
Press flat into loaf pan.
Top with sauce.
Bake at 350 degrees F for 60-75 minutes.
Take out of the oven ten minutes before the end of the bake time to pour off excess liquid.
Return to the oven to finish cooking.

Serve with mashed potatoes, gravy, peas, corn, and a tossed salad.

An excellent sandwich for lunch: leftover sliced "Meatloaf" on seeded rye bread with Gulden's spicy brown mustard and crisp lettuce.

Party Meatballs

2 lbs ground beef
8 oz Heinz tomato ketchup
12 oz ginger ale

***

Make 1-in meatballs.
Place in deep baking dish.
Cover with ketchup.
Add ginger ale.
Bake at 350 degrees F, to evaporate some of the liquid, just
until saucy.

Party Sandwiches (Grilled Cheese)

salted butter
2 slices American cheese
2 slices white bread

***

Preheat a frying pan.
Butter one side of each slice of bread.
Add two slices cheese between the slices of bread, butter side out.
Fry the sandwich on one side until browned.
Flip and fry the sandwich on the other side until browned and cheese begins to melt.
Remove sandwich to a plate.
Cut on the diagonal.

Porcupine Meatballs (Stuffed Cabbage)

1 head of cabbage
1 to 2 lb ground beef, 80% lean
a little ground pork (optional)
a little ground veal (optional)
uncooked brown rice
2 jars Prego mushroom spaghetti sauce

***

Parboil cabbage until leaves can be separated and pulled apart.
Separate the cabbage into its leaves.
Pare the toughest part of the center of each cabbage leaf, while
    maintaining each leaf intact.
Boil cabbage leaves until tender.
Combine beef, pork, veal, and rice.
Form meatballs into 2-inch logs to fit inside a rolled cabbage
    leaf.
Reserve a few meatballs to remain unwrapped.
Wrap each meatball loosely in a cabbage leaf, tucking over the
    edges.
Cover the bottom of a crock pot with spaghetti sauce.
Add a layer of wrapped meatballs.
Cover with spaghetti sauce.
Repeat layers of wrapped meatballs and spaghetti sauce, using
    all of the wrapped meatballs.
Add the unwrapped ("porcupine") meatballs.
Cover with spaghetti sauce.
Add all the leftover cabbage, if any.
Cover with spaghetti sauce.
Cook many hours, until rice is tender.

Great for kids, "Porcupine Meatballs" sounds like more fun than
"Stuffed Cabbage." The rice looks like porcupine quills but
should be cooked until it is soft.

Pork Chops

2 T vegetable oil
4 thin-cut pork chops
4 cloves garlic, sliced
1 tsp granulated cane sugar
2 tsp mushroom soy sauce
(variation) 1 C sauerkraut

***

Heat oil in cast iron skillet with raised sides.
On medium heat, fry pork chops on each side, turning
  frequently, until browned. Also turn sideways, to cook the
  fat on the sides of the pork chop in the hot oil, and make
  sure the fat also gets cooked and crisped.
Continue to cook on medium heat, until five minutes before
  meat is thoroughly cooked.
Add garlic to pan and continue to stir and cook, being careful
  not to burn garlic.
One minute before meat is thoroughly cooked, sprinkle pork
  chops with sugar and soy sauce on both sides and finish
  cooking, turning to coat pork chops evenly with sauce.

For a variation, substitute 1 cup of sauerkraut, omitting the
garlic, sugar, and soy sauce.

Pork Tenderloin

1/2 C soy sauce
2 cloves garlic, crushed
1 T grated ginger
1 T sesame oil
1 lb pork tenderloin
1/4 C honey
2 T brown sugar
4 T sesame seeds

Mix marinade: soy sauce, garlic, ginger, oil.
Marinate pork 2-24 hours in refrigerator.
Discard marinade.
Mix honey and sugar.
Roll marinated pork in honey/sugar mixture.
Roll in sesame seeds.
Roast at 450 degrees F 20 to 27 minutes, until internal temperature reaches 145 degrees.
Rest 3 minutes.
Serve hot or slice leftovers for sandwiches.

Taco Seasoning

1 T chili powder
1 T garlic powder
1 T onion powder
1 tsp cumin
1/4 tsp crushed red pepper

***

Combine seasonings: chili, garlic, onion, cumin, red pepper.
(variation) Alter the proportions of the ingredients, to taste.

Add "Taco Seasoning" to browned ground meat.
Use seasoned meat in tacos, taco salad, or "Nachos Grande."

Tacos

2 T vegetable oil, to cover skillet
1 lb lean ground beef
1 recipe "Taco Seasoning" (or ready-made Ortega brand)
1/4 C water
Ortega Taco Shells, corn (hard)
shredded sharp cheddar cheese, for topping
2 fresh plum tomatoes, diced, do not remove skin or seeds, for
    topping
1/4 head of iceberg lettuce, cut into thin strips about two inches
    long, for topping
Ortega Taco Sauce, hot, for topping

***

Preheat oven to 350 degrees F.
Spread oil to cover skillet so the meat won't stick while
    browning.
Turn stove to medium high to heat the oil.
Add ground meat to skillet.
Spread the meat over the bottom of the skillet.
Cook over medium high heat, stirring to cook evenly and to
    prevent burning or sticking to the skillet.
When meat is no longer pink, add "Taco Seasoning" and water.
    Stir to combine.
Cook over medium high heat about 2 to 5 minutes or until most
    of the water is gone.
Spread about 2 T of seasoned meat along the crease in each taco
    shell.
Place filled shells in rows on baking sheet, spaced so they do
    not touch.
Bake at 350 degrees F for about 3 minutes until hot.
Arrange taco shells upright and side by side on serving plate.
Place toppings in self-serve bowls, each with a spoon: cheese,
    tomato, lettuce, taco sauce.
Construct each taco one at a time, adding desired amount on top
    of the seasoned meat: cheese, tomato, lettuce, taco sauce.

Veal Stew

2 T olive oil
1 lb veal cubes
1 large yellow onion, diced
3 potatoes, peeled, diced
3 large carrots, peeled, cut into 1/2" rounds
1 C frozen peas, plain

***

Brown veal in olive oil on all sides.
Add onions, potatoes, and carrots.
Cover, cook on low heat until meat is done and vegetables are
    tender, about 30 minutes.
Add peas and heat 2 more minutes, until peas are tender.
Serve with buttered egg noodles.

Chocolate Filling

4 pre-melted chocolate packets
1/2 C (1 stick) salted butter, melted
8 oz sour cream
4 1/2 C (1 box) confectioner's sugar

***

Mix chocolate packets, butter, sour cream, and confectioner's
    sugar.
Place one cake layer on cake plate.
Spread half of filling on cake.
Top with second cake layer.
Spread rest of filling on top of second cake layer.
Top with third cake layer.
Ice the cake as usual.

This makes a great cake filling for a three-layer iced birthday
cake for the chocolate lover!

Chocolate Icing

2 2/3 C confectioner's sugar
1/3 to 3/4 C cocoa powder, to taste
2 T salted butter
1/3 C whole milk, just until creamy
1 tsp pure vanilla extract

***

Mix confectioner's sugar and cocoa powder.
Cream butter.
Into the butter, alternately add sugar mixture and milk, being
   careful not to add too much milk.
Add vanilla.

Cream Cheese Icing

6 T (3/4 stick) unsalted butter
6 oz Philadelphia Cream Cheese, original
3 C confectioner's sugar
1 tsp pure vanilla extract
a little whole milk, if needed

***

Bring icing ingredients to room temperature.
Cream butter and cream cheese until light and fluffy.
Beat in confectioner's sugar, vanilla, and milk, if needed.
Ice the carrot cake right away.

Crème Fraîche

2 C heavy cream
2 T buttermilk

***

Mix heavy cream and buttermilk in glass jar.
Cover with cheesecloth.
Set at warm room temperature for 8-12 hours, stirring every 5
  hours.
Cover tightly and refrigerate at least 24 hours.
Stir in flavorings, if desired, and serve.

Homemade crème fraîche can be flavored any way you like it.
Add a teaspoon of sugar or spice it up with horseradish.

Custard

2 C whole milk, for scalding
1 T cornstarch, for thickener
1/4 C granulated cane sugar, for thickener
pinch salt, for thickener
1/4 C whole milk, for thickener
2 large eggs
1 tsp pure vanilla extract

***

Scald 2 C milk by boiling in medium saucepan.
Reduce heat immediately.
Combine dry ingredients: cornstarch, sugar, salt.
Add 1/4 C whole milk to dry ingredients, to create a thickener.
Stir into the thickener: 1/2 C of the scalded milk.
Add the thickener to the rest of the scalded milk in the
    saucepan, stirring. Bring to a boil while stirring.
Turn down the heat, simmer 3 minutes, stirring. Remove from
    heat.
In mixing bowl, beat eggs, continuing to beat while adding hot
    mixture to eggs, in a stream, rather than all at once.
Add vanilla, beating to blend.
Pour back into the saucepan.
Bring just to a boil. Remove from stove.
Stir for 3 minutes.
Cool completely.

Use "Custard" in the recipe for "Trifle" or serve it by itself as a
dessert.

Gingerbread House Cement

2 C confectioner's sugar
water

***

Gradually add water to sugar just until it becomes a thick icing.

Holiday fun!

Use "Gingerbread House Cement" to stick together the walls and roof of your "Gingerbread House" and to glue on the candy decorations.

Hollandaise Sauce

1 T fresh lemon juice
2 T water
fresh black pepper, 3 to 4 twists of grinder
1/4 tsp salt
3 large egg yolks
1 1/2 sticks salted butter, cut into small chunks, softened a bit to
    almost room temperature

***

Combine juice, water, salt, and pepper
Cook on stove 5 minutes to reduce to about 2 T.
Beat the egg yolks in a pot over low heat. While continuing to
beat the yolks, pour in the reduction, in a slow, continuous, thin
stream.
Continue to beat over heat about 5 minutes.
Remove from heat.
Beat butter into yolks, a little at a time.
Serve hot.
Be very careful not to overheat the eggs or they will "cook" and
    curdle.

Spoon "Hollandaise Sauce" over steamed asparagus or "Eggs
Benedict."

Lemon Curd

3/4 C lemon juice
3/4 C granulated cane sugar
3 large eggs
1/2 C (1 stick) salted butter, cut into little pieces
1 T lemon zest

***

Combine juice, sugar, and eggs and whisk continuously over
    double boiler or over very low heat 6-10 minutes, just until
    it begins to bubble.
Remove from heat.
Add butter and zest and whisk until combined and smooth.
Refrigerate at least 1 hour in air-tight container, covering the
    surface with plastic wrap to keep out the air.
Stir again before serving.

"Lemon Curd" is wonderful served with scones.

Lemon Icing

1 T lemon juice
1/2 C plus 2 T confectioner's sugar, sifted
up to 1 T warm water

***

Whisk lemon juice into sugar.
Gradually add water just until it becomes a thick icing.
Spread icing over cooled gingerbread.
Allow to set before cutting.

This icing is delicious on "Gingerbread."

Meringue

Baking times will vary depending on the thickness of the meringue and the temperature of the dessert to which it is applied, depending on if it is still hot from the oven, room temperature, or chilled in the refrigerator.

1/4 tsp cream of tartar (Baking Option 2 or 3 only)
2 large egg whites
1/4 C granulated cane sugar

***

(Baking Option 1) Preheat oven to 200 degrees F.
(Baking Option 2) Preheat oven to 350 degrees F
(Baking Option 3) Preheat oven to 400 degrees F.

Beat egg whites to soft peaks.

(Baking Option 2) Add cream of tartar.
(Baking Option 3) Add cream of tartar.

Gradually beat in sugar to make stiff peaks.
Using a spatula, smooth meringue carefully across the top of a baked dessert, lightly, to keep the meringue fluffy and airy. Spread the meringue all the way over and firmly connect it to the edges of the pie crust or dessert top.
Create little swirled hills of meringue with peaks, by pulling bits of meringue up with the spatula. Pull each peak up until it falls off the spatula, allowing the point to drop over into a little swirl, centered on top of each little hill.

Apply the Meringue and Bake

For best results, apply the meringue to the baked dessert right

>>

Meringue (cont.)

away when it comes out of the oven, and cook immediately
while it is still hot.

If applying meringue to a cold dessert, the meringue may retain
a semi-watery layer on the bottom at the point where it
contacts the top of the dessert, and the meringue layer may
separate from the dessert.

Be sure to watch the meringue as it bakes, just until the peaks
are browned.

Bake Slowly (Option 1)

Bake at 200 degrees F about 2 to 3 hours until peaks are
browned. This will firm up the inside of the meringue, as well
as make the outside crusty.

Bake Quickly (Option 2)

To leave the insides of the meringue creamy, bake at 350
degrees F for at least 12 to 15 minutes, or until browned.

Broil Quickly (Option 3)

To broil quickly and leave the insides of the meringue soft and
creamy, set oven on Broil and place dessert on middle oven
rack. Broil at 400 degrees F for at least 3 to 4 minutes, or until
browned.

Mocha Icing

6 oz semisweet chocolate
1 T instant coffee
2 tsp very hot tap water
1/2 lb salted butter
1 tsp pure vanilla extract
1 1/4 C confectioner's sugar

***

Melt chocolate, cool.
Mix instant coffee and very hot tap water.
Beat butter until fluffy.
Add vanilla, beat until fluffy.
Add confectioner's sugar, beat until smooth and creamy.
Stir in Chocolate and Instant Coffee.

Orange Glaze

1 1/4 C sugar
1/2 C orange juice
1 tsp orange rind
1/2 tsp orange extract

***

Whisk ingredients together in saucepan.
Bring to a boil.
Allow to cool.
Drizzle over top of bundt cake.

This glaze is delicious on bundt cake.

Sesame Sauce

1 C chicken broth
1/2 C water
1/4 C rice wine vinegar
2 T dark soy sauce
2 T sesame oil
1 tsp chili paste
1 C sugar
2 T corn starch

***

Mix chicken broth, water, rice wine vinegar, soy sauce, sesame
    oil, and chili paste.
Stir in sugar and cornstarch.
Bring to a boil.
Simmer 5 minutes, or until thickened.

Whipped Cream

8 oz heavy cream
2 T sugar
4 T chocolate syrup (optional)

***

For best results in whipping cream, the bowl and the mixer's
   metal beaters must be absolutely clean, dry, and cold.
Chill (covered) both the bowl and the beaters in the freezer,
   until cold.
Beat heavy cream with electric mixer on highest setting, until
   whipped into fluffy peaks.
Gently fold in sugar and chocolate (optional) with rubber
   spatula.
Serve immediately.

Homemade whipped cream can be flavored any way you like it.
Use as a topping on pancakes or waffles, pies, strawberry
shortcake, ice cream, pound cake, or gingerbread; or use
chocolate whipped cream as icing on chocolate cake.

White Sauce

2 T salted butter
2 T white wheat flour
2 C whole milk
more of these ingredients, as needed

***

Melt butter in cast iron pan. Sprinkle flour over butter.
Cook over low heat while stirring constantly, until flour just
begins to brown slightly.
For a brown gravy base, continue cooking the flour until well
browned. Brown the flour well, just continue with the next
step of adding milk gradually.
Continue to cook while stirring in a little of the milk, continuing
to stir until smooth.
While continuing to cook, stir in the rest of the milk gradually, a
little at a time, continuing to stir until smooth after each
addition.
Continue until all of the milk has been added.
To thicken the white sauce, continue heating until bubbling and
cook until volume is reduced to desired thickness.
More flour can be added if needed to thicken the sauce, but the
goal is to avoid lumpiness, which can be caused by adding
flour to the sauce as it is cooking. To avoid clumps, first
place the extra flour into a lidded container along with a
spoonful or so of cold water. Shake it vigorously to soak the
flour and to break up any flour clumps.
After adding the last of the flour, the sauce must be cooked for
at least an additional 10 minutes, to make sure that the flour
is thoroughly cooked.
Use more of each of the ingredients to make a larger volume of
"White Sauce.

Homemade white sauce can be flavored any way you like it and
is used as a base for sauces, gravies, and other dishes. A family
favorite is "Chicken, Rice, and Peas."

Shirley Temple (glass)

orange juice
cranberry juice
ginger ale
simple syrup
toothpick
maraschino cherry
orange
pineapple
mini straw
pink paper umbrella

***

Pour drink ingredients into glass.
Stick a toothpick with a cherry, orange slice, and pineapple.
Garnish with mini straw, fruited toothpick, and pink umbrella.

Bloody Mary (tall glass)

1 tsp celery salt
2 wedges lemon
2 wedges lime
6-10 ice cubes
2 oz vodka
4 oz tomato juice
2 dashes Tabasco sauce
2 tsp horseradish
1 pinch celery salt
1 pinch pepper
1 pinch smoked paprika
ice cubes
1 stalk celery
1 lime wedge

***

Sprinkle celery salt onto small plate.
Moisten edge of glass by rubbing with lemon or lime wedge.
Dip glass upside-down into plate of celery salt to coat edge.
Fill glass with ice cubes.
Squeeze juice from lemon and lime wedges into shaker.
Drop lemon and lime wedges into shaker.
Add vodka, juice, Tabasco, horseradish, Worcestershire, celery
    salt, pepper, and paprika to shaker.
Fill shaker with ice cubes.
Shake gently.
Strain into glass.
Garnish with celery and lime.

Margarita (Pitcher)

water, for wetting glass
1 tsp salt, for dipping glass
crushed ice
1 can frozen limeade
6 oz tequila
2 oz triple sec
paper umbrella

***

Combine in blender: ice, limeade, tequila, triple sec.
Sprinkle salt onto plate.
Wet rim of glass with water, then dip into plate of salt.
Pour drink into glasses rimmed with salt.
Garnish with paper umbrella.

Mimosa (Pitcher)

1 bottle champagne
3/4 C Triple Sec
3 C orange juice
orange round

***

Gently pour champagne into pitcher.
Stir in Triple Sec and juice.
Garnish with orange round.

Mojito (Pitcher)

1/2 C sugar
36 leaves fresh mint
3 limes, quartered
1 C rum
1 liter club soda
lime round
sprig fresh mint

***

Muddle sugar with mint in pitcher.
Add limes and muddle.
Stir in rum.
Add club soda and stir.
Garnish with lime and mint.

Piña Colada (tall glass)

4 chunks fresh pineapple
2 tsp superfine sugar
1 part fresh pineapple juice
1 1/2 parts fresh coconut water
2 parts light rum
ice cubes
crushed ice
fresh pineapple

***

Muddle pineapple in shaker with sugar.
Stir in juice and coconut water to dissolve the sugar.
Add rum.
Fill shaker to top with ice cubes.
Shake until frosted.
Strain into tall glass filled with crushed ice.
Garnish with fresh pineapple.

Rum and Coke (glass)

1 part rum
3 parts cola, chilled

***

Add rum and coke to glass.

Screwdriver (glass)

1 part vodka
3 parts orange juice, chilled

***

Mix vodka and orange juice in a glass.

Sloe Gin Fizz (glass)

2 oz sloe gin
1 oz lemon juice
1 tsp simple syrup
1 C ice
2 ice cubes
4 oz club soda
lemon slice

***

Shake sloe gin, lemon juice, simple syrup, and ice.
Strain into a frozen highball glass.
Add ice cubes and club soda.
Garnish with lemon slice.

Strawberry Daquiri (Pitcher)

6 C ice
1/2 C sugar
4 oz frozen strawberries
1 oz lime juice
4 oz lemon juice
6 oz rum
2 oz lemon-lime soda
fresh strawberry
pink paper umbrella

***

Blend ice, sugar, and strawberries in a blender.
Add juices, rum, and soda.
Blend until smooth.
Pour into glasses.
Garnish with a fresh strawberry and a pink umbrella.

Tequila Sunrise (glass)

3/4 C orange juice
1 jigger tequila
1/2 jigger grenadine
toothpick
maraschino cherry
orange slice
pink paper umbrella

***

Mix orange juice and tequila in glass.
Carefully pour grenadine to slide to the bottom of the glass so
the layer with orange juice and tequila is floating on top.
Garnish a toothpick with a cherry and orange slice.
Garnish with pink umbrella.

Cherries Flambeau

At the end of every delicious dinner fit for a king, which was every home-cooked meal we ever had, my father would anticipate the fabulous dessert of his dreams.

"Bring on the Cherries Flambeau!" he would exclaim, a triumphant shout to signify that the best is yet to come.

True Cherries Flambeau never materialized. My mother was supposed to be flattered that my father considered her a cook par excellence, that nothing could possibly serve to finish such a fine meal as my mom had prepared other than the grandest ending known to delight the culinary masters.

Cherries Flambeau? She was a full-time school administrator with the public school system, a full-time volunteer in the community, a full-time bridge player with her best friends, a full-time mother of eight children, and a full-time life partner for my dad. When my mom wanted to impress her darlings with a special dessert, we saw slender, round slices of banana floating in our strawberry Jell-O. For company, she would add bits of cut-up maraschino cherries. It might have been nice if the fancy copper Jell-O mold in the shape of a fish ever came down off its hook above the kitchen sink, but it took too much time to polish.

We had dessert after dinner every night, and every night it was a surprise. We all clung to the dream that, one day, we'd see a glow coming from the kitchen after dinner. My mom always disappeared beyond the swing half-doors leading to the kitchen in order to bring out the day's dessert as a surprise. My dad added his enthusisastic dialog to add to the suspense.

>>

Cherries Flambeau (cont.)

My parents were frugal and could not afford wasted food. They needed their children to eat all the food they put on the table. I ate everything on my plate so I would be member of the Clean Plate Club. Only members were allowed dessert.

Though I usually ate with gusto, one day we had liver and onions for dinner.

Liver and onions? It lived up to its ill repute!

It took a great deal of struggle, but I choked it down. Today might be the day dessert would be Cherries Flambeau.

Recipe Titles

AUTHOR

"It's amazing to think Susanna Lee hasn't changed a bit since her yearbook photo."

—*no one ever*

Susanna Lee is a writer from the rural area in northern New Jersey where drivers stop to give bears crossing the road the right of way. Her work has been published in *brevitas, First Literary Review – East, Sensations Magazine, The Red Wheelbarrow, The Stillwater Review, The World According to Twitter, Voices From Here 2,* and her first book of poetry, *Sunrise Mountain,* 2015, which is now out of print. The volumes of Lee's collected works, published by Rose Mason Press as the *Cubist Poetry Series,* offer the reader a kaleidoscopic view of her writing. The first printing, in 2021, was a "Pandemic Panic!" version. The author was not sure she would not be touched by the contagion, but wanted her admittedly imperfect words to survive: she set them free in haste. She has since reworked the books: proofread and edited, corrected spacing errors, and vanquished typos – at least, most of them – for this 2022 printing. *Snow Balls* consists of short stories, many autobiographical. *Great Blue Heron* is a collection of 5-7-5 haiku arranged in mini-chapbooks on various themes, such as pop culture, nursery rhymes, and art history—and with a bonus: haiku suitable for including in greeting cards on every special occasion. Lee's poems sonnet length and shorter appear in *Twisted Carrot*, poems longer than one page are in *God Laughs*, and her one-page poems are in *My Husband's Roses.* Lee's family recipes are preserved in *Fluffy Muffins*, which includes a section of instructions in kitchen basics for new cooks. Lee celebrates her love of music in bringing to print a newly discovered manuscript written eighty years ago by a friend's uncle, Jerome Bengis. Included with the found monograph, *Beethoven and His Nine Symphonies,* was a Forward by professor of music Edward Dickinson. Bengis' nephew Michael Bengis added a Preface. Lee added an Introduction and an Afterword and gave the book the title *Genius in 9 Symphonies.*

GRATITUDE

So much love has gone into the preparation of the foods in these recipes over the years by so many caring cooks and nurturers, who have all been part of the inspiration for my wish to share what I have learned about cooking, but I am most grateful to my mother for making excellent choices in feeding our family. Thank you to all family and friends whose nutritious and delicious foods I have enjoyed and who have shared recipes and demonstrated cooking techniques.

I am also grateful to my cousin CJ Rhoads, who has believed in my writing from the beginning and helped me bring my poetry, stories, and this family cookbook to print.

Published by Rose Mason Press

Sunrise Mountain: Haiku and Other Poetry
by Susanna Lee

Twisted Carrot: Petite Poems
by Susanna Lee

My Husband's Roses: One-Page Poems
by Susanna Lee

God Laughs: Longer Poems
by Susanna Lee

Great Blue Heron: Haiku
by Susanna Lee

Snow Balls: Short Stories
by Susanna Lee

Fluffy Muffins: Recipes for My Peeps
by Susanna Lee

Genius in 9 Symphonies: How Beethoven Reinvented Music
by Jerome Bengis

Please gift a Rose Mason Press title to someone you love.

Made in the USA
Middletown, DE
26 March 2022